On this Day . . .

A YEAR IN THE LIFE
OF NASHVILLE
AND
MIDDLE TENNESSEE

On this Day . . .

A Year in the Life of Nashville and Middle Tennessee

by

James A. Crutchfield

Cool Springs Press
Franklin, Tennessee

Published by
Cool Springs Press
Franklin, Tn 37064

ISBN 0-9640392-1-4

Printed by Vaughan Printing

Printed in the United States of America

Cover design by June Steckler

To all of the people of Nashville--
Past, Present, and Future

Contents

A WORD TO THE READER

The book you are about to read is a compilation of interesting events that have occurred during the long and varied history of Nashville, Tennessee. In the pages herein, you will find 366 episodes of local history, one for every day of the year, including February 29. Some of the incidents depicted were of vital importance to the evolution and growth of the city, while others are merely interesting tidbits of history that, when taken alone, are of little significance.

In order to illustrate some of the events in the book, I have had to rely on several sources. Each picture is individually acknowledged, and I owe a debt of gratitude to those various people, institutions, and book publishers listed.

Read on then and learn a little bit about the life and times of our fair city. I hope that you will experience as much fun reading this book as I did while researching and writing it.

James A. Crutchfield

A BRIEF HISTORY OF NASHVILLE

Prior to permanent occupation by English-speaking settlers from the Watauga settlements in what is now East Tennessee, the Nashville region served as home for an assortment of prehistoric American Indian peoples. The high level of technology attained by one of these cultures, the Mississippian, far surpassed that of any other native group north of Mexico during its long existence from 700 A. D until 1500 A. D. Hundreds of years later, several historic tribes of Indians--the Cherokee, Chickasaw, and Shawnee--used the rich Nashville basin as a vast hunting ground that was held in communal trust for the benefit of all.

During the time that French traders frequented the valley of the Cumberland River around the end of the seventeenth century and the beginning of the eighteenth, a French trading post was established upon the site of Nashville. Later, in 1760, Timothy Demonbreun, a French-Canadian trader, made his home in a cave high above the Cumberland River. Several parties of "long hunters" frequented the area between the years 1769 and 1779, in search of the abundant supply of wild animals. Eventually, word of mouth tales about the bountiful game and luxuriant land in the region along the Cumberland River convinced Watauga leaders to send permanent settlement parties to the Bluffs, or the French Lick, as the site of Nashville was then called.

The James Robertson-John Donelson parties arrived in 1779-1780 to establish Fort Nashborough, which four years later became Nashville. Harsh weather, the untamed land, and frequent violent attacks by hostile Indians made life during the first few years of habitation on the Cumberland almost unbearable. However, by 1795, peace had finally come to the frontier, and some semblance of order prevailed in the settlements.

Civilization was not long coming to Nashville. Lardner Clark opened the first store in town in 1783, between present-day First and Second Avenues, North. A court house and jail were built on the Public Square in this same vicinity in 1784. In 1786, the first school and church west of the Cumberland Mountains were opened just east of Nashville in the Haysborough community. By the turn of the century, Nashville could vie with any other western settlement removed so far from the mainstream of national events. In 1820, Nashville's population was 3,400, and the town was well on its way to becoming an important element in the history of the old Southwest.

The period from 1820 through the 1850s was one of dynamic growth in Nashville. The first bridge to span the Cumberland River was built in 1823. Construction in the area around the Public Square expanded rapidly. The State Capitol building was begun in 1845, and several downtown churches, some still standing today, were completed during this period.

During these four decades, Nashvillians observed several of their neighbors climb to prominence in national and international affairs. Andrew Jackson became President of the United States in 1829, serving two terms. In 1836, former Nashvillian, Sam Houston, stepped into the president's office of the newly organized Republic of Texas. James K. Polk became U. S. president in 1845, and in 1856, William Walker, who had left his home on present-day Fourth Avenue, North, years earlier, was elected president of Nicaragua. John Bell conducted an unsuccessful presidential campaign against Abraham Lincoln and Stephen Douglas in 1860. Clearly, as the War Between the States rapidly approached, Nashville had established itself as a rising star in the Old South.

The War was already a year old in April, 1862, when Nashvillians watched Union troops occupy their city. In December, 1864, an abortive attempt by Confederate General John Bell Hood to recapture Nashville with his battle-weary Army of Tennessee left the city in Union hands until the end of the conflict. Then followed the horror of Reconstruction, ironically imposed by another Tennessean and frequent visitor to Nashville, President Andrew Johnson.

An era of relative prosperity followed Reconstruction. Although railroads and steamboats first frequented Nashville before the War, these two methods of transportation and travel came into their own in the years that followed it. Gas lighting became increasingly popular, and in 1882, the city's residents were introduced to the electric light bulb. At about the same time, the telephone became a rare luxury, but by 1884, happy customers boasted six hundred of the devices. With all these conveniences and a population of nearly 81,000 by 1900, Nashville was poised to make the leap into the Modern Age.

The Twentieth Century brought many changes to Nashville. Here, like in many other parts of the nation, the simplicity of farm and small town living was rapidly giving way to the pressures and complexities of urban existence. Mass production replaced individual craftsmanship, and Nashvillians found themselves in the midst of an era of industrialization and high finance.

Two insurance companies that would one day stand among the giants of the industry were founded in the first decade of the Twentieth Century. An automobile, the Marathon, was manufactured in the city between 1910 and 1914. During World War One, Du Pont's Old Hickory powder plant supplied three-quarters of a million pounds of gunpowder to the Allied armies in Europe every day. By the time the United States prepared for battle on the eve of World War Two, Nashville had become one of the South's largest cities, with a population of nearly 168,000 residents.

First the threat, then the reality, of global war shook Nashville out of its post-Depression slump. A wartime economy spurred new growth, and Nashville manufacturers supplied the war effort with airplane parts, weaponry, and other essential materiel. A revitalization of the downtown area began in the 1950s with the advent of urban renewal. In 1962, the governments of Nashville and Davidson County combined their resources giving rise to Metropolitan Nashville.

Today, with a population of more than one-half million people -- with several hundred thousand more residing in the surrounding counties, but working in the city--Nashville has become one of the nation's leaders in the music industry, in the hospital services field, in publishing and printing, and in tourism. Call it what you will--Athens of the South; Music City, U.S.A.; or Financial Capital of the Southeast--Nashville stands ever ready to fulfill its time-honored role as one of America's foremost cities.

On this Day . . .

A YEAR IN THE LIFE
OF NASHVILLE
AND

MIDDLE TENNESSEE

JANUARY 1, 1866

The United States Post Office introduces home-delivered mail in Nashville. Jerry Buckley is the city's first letter-carrier, but before the year is over, seven more walking postmen will be hired. The system of mail-sorting is uncomplicated. A dispatcher simply calls the addressee's name, and when one of the carriers claims the letter for his route, the mail is dropped down a chute that delivers it into the correct postman's bag.

JANUARY 2, 1869

The section of Nashville that lies east of the Cumberland River and bound by Shelby Avenue, the river, Berry and Cowan Streets, and South 10th Street is incorporated into a separate city called Edgefield. The residents of the new entity elect their own mayor and run the town as a sister community to Nashville. In time, the closeness of the two cities makes the separation impractical, and on February 6, 1880, Nashville re-annexes Edgefield.

JANUARY 3, 1807

As several Nashville citizens endure the icy winds blowing across the Cumberland River, they watch intently as an effigy of former Vice-president of the United States Aaron Burr is burned in front of the court house on the Public Square. Burr, who has visited Nashville frequently in the past and has many friends here, is now a wanted man, accused of treason for aiding Spanish authorities in a move to separate Tennessee from the rest of the country.

Colonel Luke Lea and the team assembled to kidnap Kaiser Wilhelm during the opening days of 1919. Seated left to right: Captain Leland S. McPhail of Nashville, later the controversial owner of the Brooklyn Dodgers and the New York Yankees; Colonel Luke Lea; Captain Thomas P. Henderson of Franklin; and Lieutenant Ellsworth Brown, hometown unknown. Standing left to right: Sergeant Dan Reilly of Williamson County; Sergeant Toliver, hometown unknown; Sergeant Owen Johnston of Williamson County; and Corporal Marmaduke Clokey, hometown unknown.

JANUARY 4, 1919

Luke Lea, a former United States senator from Nashville and currently a colonel in the American army in Europe, formulates a plan to kidnap the German Kaiser, Wilhelm. He recruits several other Tennesseans, including Captain Tom Henderson and Sergeants Dan Reilly and Owen Johnston from Williamson County. Lea receives a *carte blanche* pass, authorized by the Queen, to enter Holland. After a wild ride across the Dutch countryside, the Americans reach Wilhelm's castle, but fail to capture the German.

General Andrew Jackson as he appeared during the War of 1812.

JANUARY 5, 1900

Grocery prices in Nashville: Ham, $ .10 a pound; potatoes, $ .75 a bushel; eggs, $ .17 a dozen; hens, 6 cents each.

JANUARY 6, 1818

Three years after his decisive victory over the British at New Orleans, Andrew Jackson, once again called upon by his government to defend the country's frontier in the wake of the First Seminole War, suggests to President James Monroe that the United States take possession of Spanish Florida. The U. S. eventually purchases Florida, and Jackson serves as governor for a brief time.

JANUARY 7, 1838

Francis Tomes, a British banker, is impressed with Nashville. As he prepares to leave the city the following day, he remarks, "Everybody knows that good society is in Nashville. Here is to be found in one person the generosity of the Southerner and the industry of the Northerner. Unlike every other western town I have been in, the streets are not muddy. It is, therefore, no sin to wear boots."

JANUARY 8, 1815

Andrew Jackson becomes a national hero when the Nashvillian-- accompanied by a mixed command of Tennesseans, Kentuckians, pirates, blacks, and Indians-- defeat the British Army at New Orleans in the last battle of the War of 1812. When British General Edward Pakenham's elite soldiers attack, they are mowed down rapidly by Jackson's marksmen. Seven hundred British troops are killed, including General

Andrew Jackson and his men at the Battle of New Orleans.

Pakenham, along with fourteen hundred more wounded. American losses are eight men killed and thirteen wounded.

JANUARY 9, 1866

Fisk School, named in honor of General Clinton B. Fisk, the head of the Freedmen's Bureau of Tennessee, is opened in

North Nashville. Established to provide educational opportunities for freed slaves after the War Between the States, Fisk becomes Fisk University in 1867. A few years later, the renowned Fisk Jubilee Singers will travel the world raising money for the school.

JANUARY 10, 1946

Nashvillian John DeWitt, a lieutenant-colonel in the United States Army stationed at the Evans Signal Laboratories in Belmar, New Jersey, makes humankind's first direct contact with the Moon, via radar. At 11:58 A.M., the oscilloscope used during the experiments begins to emit tiny flicks of light, denoting that radar beams have already traveled the 239,000 miles between the Earth and the Moon and back again.

JANUARY 11, 1781

Charlotte, wife of Nashville's founder, James Robertson, gives birth to the first white child born in the Cumberland Settlements. The boy, named Felix, will become one of Nashville's leading citizens as a physician, the city's mayor, and president of the Medical Society of Tennessee. Before he dies in 1865,

Felix Robertson, first white child born in Nashville.

Dr. Robertson will witness the growth of Nashville from a stockaded frontier post containing a few score residents to one of the South's leading and most progressive cities.

JANUARY 12, 1918

The mercury in Nashville falls to seventeen degrees below zero, making this day one of the coldest in the city's history.

JANUARY 13, 1894

Following the deaths of several Nashville residents from small-pox, city fathers vote an appropriation of $5,000--today's equivalent of nearly $100,000--to fight the disease.

JANUARY 14, 1893

Vice-president of the United States Adlai E. Stevenson, visits Nashville and addresses the State Legislature on Capitol Hill.

JANUARY 15, 1786

Although the exact date is lost in history, Colonel John Donelson, co-founder of Nashville, is killed by unknown assailants while traveling from the Kentucky settlements to Mansker's Station and his awaiting family. Somewhere, during mid-January, just north of today's Tennessee-Kentucky border, Donelson meets two young men, and the three of them continue toward Nashville. A few days later, the two travelers arrive in town and tell sorrowful residents that their friend was killed by Indians. To this day, Donelson's death remains a mystery.

JANUARY 16, 1781

Shortly after midnight, Indians attack Freeland's Station, one of the early forts built in the Nashville area and located near today's Werthan Industries on Eighth Avenue, North. James Robertson has just arrived at Freeland's from a Kentucky trip and is visiting his wife and infant son. Only eleven defenders fight off about fifty Indians before reinforcements from Fort Nashborough arrive.

JANUARY 17, 1979

In Nashville, Lamar Alexander assumes the office of Tennessee governor three days early when federal prosecutors warn officials that current Governor Ray Blanton might continue to free prisoners in an effort to protect himself in a wide-spread "pardons" scandal. When he hears of the news from a television bulletin, Blanton tells reporters that "I am saddened and hurt for the state of Tennessee that this clandestine action has taken place this evening." Blanton is eventually convicted and serves prison time.

Governor Lamar Alexander

JANUARY 18, 1792

Three sons of Colonel Valentine Sevier, an early settler in today's Montgomery County, leave their father's fort at the mouth of the Red River near today's city of Clarksville. Their destination is Nashville to heed James Robertson's call to arms against marauding Indians. Toward the middle of the day, as they proceed in their canoe up the Cumberland River, the three young men are attacked by Indians. All three Seviers are killed.

Sevier's Blockhouse

JANUARY 19, 1862

Brigadier-general Felix Zollicoffer, a Nashville journalist, former United States Congressman, and advocate for States Rights, is killed in action on the north bank of the Cumberland River during the Battle of Mill Springs, Kentucky, fought between today's towns of Somerset and Monticello. Zollicoffer is wearing a white rain coat, and in the shrouded visibility caused by heavy rainfall, both Confederate and Union troops are confused about his real identity.

JANUARY 20, 1902

The National Prohibition Amendment becomes effective. In an advertisement in the *Nashville Banner*, the local chapter of the Anti-Saloon League proclaims that "Bolshevism flourishes in wet soil. Failure to enforce prohibition in Russia was followed by Bolshevism. Failure to enforce Prohibition HERE will encourage Bolshevism, disrespect for law and INVITE INDUSTRIAL DISASTER."

JANUARY 21, 1876

For the second time in nine days, fire destroys several buildings in downtown Nashville. Today's conflagration is on South Market Street. On January 12, the entire Luck's Block of commercial buildings on Church Street was likewise razed by flames.

JANUARY 22, 1829

Thirty-five year old Governor Sam Houston--formerly a Nashville district attorney, adjutant-general of Tennessee, and U. S. Congressman--marries eighteen year old Eliza Allen of Gallatin. Within twelve weeks the marriage is over. Houston resigns as governor and leaves Nashville for the West, never to return to the city as a resident. Eliza Allen returns to her father's home in Gallatin. The couple officially divorce two years later. Houston eventually migrates to Texas, where he becomes the Republic's president in 1836.

Sam Houston as an older man after he had left Tennessee and made his mark in Texas.

JANUARY 23, 1893

Nashville resident, Howell E. Jackson, a son-in-law of Belle Meade Plantation's owner, General William Giles Harding, is appointed associate justice on the United States Supreme Court by President Benjamin Harrison.

JANUARY 24, 1892

The sins of the theater and the idle pastime called "dancing" are condemned in a sermon at McKendree Methodist Church in downtown Nashville.

JANUARY 25, 1910

The Hermitage Hotel, located at the corner of Sixth Avenue and Union Street, opens for business. Designed by Columbia, Tennessee, architect, J. Edwin Carpenter, the hotel incorporates local marble in its magnificent lobby. Prints depicting life during the War Between the States by former Nashville artist, Gilbert Gaul, adorn the lobby walls.

JANUARY 26, 1935

Floods across Tennessee affect Nashville when the Cumberland River and many of its tributaries overflow their banks. The resultant damage to the region is estimated to be in the millions of dollars.

JANUARY 27, 1830

In a great senatorial debate in Washington, D. C., former Williamson County resident and frequent visitor to Nashville, Thomas Hart Benton, now a U. S. senator from Missouri-- argues vehemently against restricting the sale of public lands in the West. Benton, who has not yet acquired his reputation as the Senate's leading advocate for westward expansion, accuses his Eastern opponents of bowing to industrial interests who favor the land restrictions in order to capitalize on cheap labor pools back home.

President James K. Polk

JANUARY 28, 1845

James K. Polk--Columbia resident, former speaker of the United States House of Representatives, and former governor of Tennessee--leaves his home for the long trip to Washington, D. C. In March, Polk will be inaugurated president of the United States. A frequent visitor to Nashville, especially to the Hermitage, home of his friend, Andrew Jackson, Polk will spend the night in Franklin and arrive in Nashville the following day.

The original St. Thomas Hospital on Hayes Street, as it appeared in 1907.

JANUARY 29, 1902

At the unheard of cost of $200,000, St. Thomas Hospital opens the doors of its new facility on Hayes Street. The new building takes the place of an older one, formerly the home of Judge Jacob McGavock Dickinson. The daily charge for a room is one dollar.

JANUARY 30, 1835

Andrew Jackson becomes the first American president to be the target of an assassination attempt. As "Old Hickory" leaves the funeral for a congressional friend at the U. S. Capitol Building, a disgruntled house painter aims two pistols at the president, but miraculously, both misfire.

JANUARY 31, 1951

The "Blizzard of '51" begins with freezing rain which soon turns to sleet. Before it is over, the storm, judged by some to be the worst in Nashville's history, will completely disable the city, leaving many residents without heat and electricity for weeks. Schools and businesses close, and transportation is non-existent.

FEBRUARY 1, 1895

Judge Jacob McGavock Dickinson is nominated by President Grover Cleveland to fill the position of Assistant Attorney General of the United States. Later, Judge Dickinson serves as U. S. Secretary of War in President William Howard Taft's administration.

FEBRUARY 2, 1905

For the first time since 1893, the Cumberland River at Nashville freezes over. Icy temperatures grip the mid-state region.

FEBRUARY 3, 1884

Frank Andrews, the first air officer ever to command an entire theater of operations, is born in Nashville. During World War Two, General Andrews will succeed General Dwight D. Eisenhower to the position of commander of all American army forces in Europe, a job he will hold until his death in an air accident in 1943. Andrews Air Force Base in Maryland will be named in his honor.

FEBRUARY 4, 1909

The manufacture of liquor becomes illegal in Tennessee.

FEBRUARY 5, 1902

The custom of charging highway users a fee, or "toll," to be used in defraying the expense of road upkeep and maintenance faces a dismal future as the last tollgate in Davidson County is vacated by the Franklin Turnpike Company.

FEBRUARY 6, 1862

General Lloyd Tilghman, the Confederate commander of Fort Henry on the Tennessee River and Fort Donelson on the Cumberland, surrenders Henry to Union forces under Admiral A. H. Foote. Fort Henry's fall greatly jeopardizes the safety of its sister installation, Fort Donelson, and leaves a hole in the northern defenses of Nashville, situated only a few miles to the south.

FEBRUARY 7, 1849

President-elect Zachary Taylor, who in less than a month will succeed Tennessee's own James K. Polk in the White House, deboards from a steamboat that has carried him up the Cumberland River to Nashville. Unlike Polk, a Democrat, Taylor is a Whig, yet he has carried Tennessee over the Democratic candidate, Lewis Cass, by more than six thousand votes in the recent election.

Zachary Taylor, popular Mexican War hero and president-elect of the United States.

FEBRUARY 8, 1896

A Nashville breeder sells several homing pigeons to the Associated Press who will use the birds to transport news releases to the United States from the ongoing revolution in Cuba.

FEBRUARY 9, 1861

In a vote that will pit pro-Union East Tennesseans against residents living in pro-slavery Middle and West Tennessee, the mandate is for the state *not* to secede from the United States. When the votes are finally counted, the tally is 69,387 against secession and 57,798 for leaving the Union. For the time being, Tennesseans have elected to stay a part of the United States. Four months later, feelings will be decidedly different.

FEBRUARY 10, 1865

Almost two months after General John Bell Hood fails to recapture Nashville for the South, Confederate and Union forces skirmish near Triune, in neighboring Williamson County.

FEBRUARY 11, 1862

As Admiral Foote moves his gunships down the Tennessee River, up the Ohio, and turns them into the mouth of the Cumberland to lay siege at Fort Donelson, General Simon Bolivar Buckner arrives in the neighborhood to assist in the strengthening of the Confederate defenses.

Confederate General
Simon Bolivar Buckner.

FEBRUARY 12, 1892

Edward Ward Carmack, a controversial newspaperman who will later serve in the United States House of Representatives and the U. S. Senate for ten years, resigns his duties as editor of the Nashville *Daily American* to assume the editorship of the Memphis *Commercial Appeal.*

FEBRUARY 13, 1851

The first gas-lit street lights in Nashville are demonstrated to an awed public at the corner of Second Avenue, North and the Public Square.

FEBRUARY 14, 1862

Two Union gunboats and four ironclads open fire on the Confederate garrison at Fort Donelson, several miles downstream from Nashville. During this early encounter in the War Between the States, one of the defenders remarks, "Pandemonium itself would hardly have been more appalling."

FEBRUARY 15, 1791

Five years before Tennessee attains statehood, the territorial

governor, William Blount, appoints Andrew Jackson to the position of attorney-general for the Mero District, a political division which includes Nashville.

William Blount, governor of the Territory of the United States, South of the River Ohio, commonly called the Southwest Territory, the precursor to Tennessee.

Fort Donelson under attack by Union gunboats.

FEBRUARY 16, 1862

A rumor, shortly afterwards confirmed as fact, sends chills through the hearts of many Nashvillians. Fort Donelson, the last outpost protecting the city from a northern invasion, has fallen to the Union Army.

FEBRUARY 17, 1903

A severe blizzard hits Nashville and the surrounding country-side, plummeting temperatures and making travel hazardous.

FEBRUARY 18, 1862

Nashvillians, fearful of the imminent Union invasion of the city, destroy the bridges across the Cumberland River. The wires that support the suspension bridge are cut, causing the structure to crash into the icy river one hundred feet below. The railroad bridge--a wooden, covered edifice--is set afire and burns all night. Confederate troops prepare to leave the city.

FEBRUARY 19, 1867

At Washington, D. C., in a speech before the United States Senate, Tennessee Senator Joseph Fowler, a Union sympathizer during the War Between the States, endorses the need for continued Federal military sovereignty over the South, including his home state. Fowler also favors abolishing the rights of un-reconstructed Southerners to vote.

FEBRUARY 20, 1918

Mrs. Florenz Ziegfeld brings her husband's world-famous Ziegfeld Follies to the Ryman Auditorium. Billed as the "World's Greatest Musical Show," the Follies star Fannie Brice and Willie and Eugene Howard.

Theater poster for Mrs. Ziegfeld's new edition of the Follies.

FEBRUARY 21, 1854

The Tennessee Legislature awards Mark Cockrill of Nashville a gold medal for his contributions to animal husbandry. A nephew of Nashville's founder, James Robertson, the sixty-six year old Cockrill has worked for years on his farm in the vicinity of today's Centennial Park to improve the quality of wool. In 1851, wool from his fine Merino sheep won first place in the London World's Fair.

FEBRUARY 22, 1848

Using the newly invented telegraph, Henry O'Reilly of Louisville, Kentucky sends his well wishes to Nashvillians, marking the first ever use of the telegraph in Nashville.

FEBRUARY 23, 1862

At nine o'clock in the morning, Union troops pull into Edgefield, just across the Cumberland River from Nashville. The city's mayor, R. B. Cheatham, is summoned to the Union camp and informed of the terms of surrender by Union General Don Carlos Buell. As hundreds of citizens and Confederate soldiers flee the city, news is received that President Abraham Lincoln has just appointed Andrew Johnson to the post of military governor of Tennessee.

FEBRUARY 24, 1865

John Beall, fiance of Martha O'Bryan, is hanged by Union authorities in New York. Miss O'Bryan vows to devote the rest of her life in service to others. The Martha O'Bryan Community Center in Nashville is named in her honor.

FEBRUARY 25, 1862

After meeting once again with Union General Don Carlos Buell in Edgefield, Mayor R. B. Cheatham returns to Nashville and issues a proclamation of surrender. "There is every assurance of safety and protection to the people, both in their persons and in their property. I therefore respectfully request that business be resumed, and all our citizens, of every trade and profession, pursue their regular vocations," reads the announcement. With the surrender of Nashville, Union forces will occupy most of Middle Tennessee until the end of the War.

FEBRUARY 26, 1856

The Hume School, located on the site of today's Hume-Fogg School at Eighth Avenue, North and Broad Street, is opened as the first public school in Nashville. Named in honor of Alfred E. Hume, "the father of the Nashville school system," the institution starts a tradition of educational excellence in the city.

The original Hume School.

FEBRUARY 27, 1979

NLT Corporation of Nashville acquires Great Southern Life Insurance Company and becomes the largest business in Tennessee in terms of assets and revenues.

FEBRUARY 28, 1813

Somewhere on the Natchez Trace between Natchez, Mississippi and Nashville, while returning his Tennessee troops home, General Andrew Jackson earns his nickname, "Old Hickory," when one of his soldiers compares him to the toughness of hickory wood.

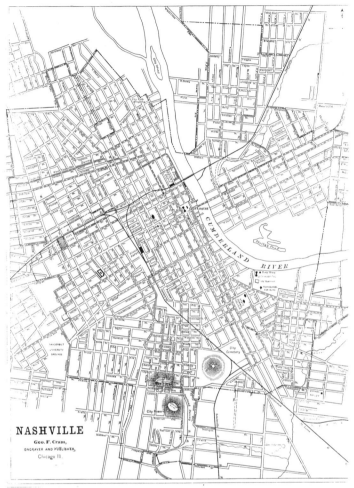

Map of Nashville around the turn of the twentieth century.

FEBRUARY 29, 1900

The city of Nashville covers ten square miles and boasts 140 miles of streets, seventy-two miles of streetcar lines, and fifty-nine miles of sewers. Population stands at 80,865. Tennessee's population, in the meantime, has risen to a few thousand over two million.

MARCH 1, 1958

Nashville-born Cardinal Samuel Stritch, a one-time parish priest in his native city, and, later, the Archbishop of Chicago, is appointed Pro-Prefect of the Congregation for the Propagation of the Faith by Pope Pius XII. Stritch dies three months after his appointment, but before he can assume his duties in Rome.

MARCH 2, 1902

Prince Henry of Prussia, the brother of Kaiser Wilhelm of Germany, visits Nashville.

MARCH 3, 1821

J. D. Steele, a New Yorker who is visiting Nashville, dines with Andrew Jackson at the Hermitage. Although Steele is generally unimpressed with Nashville, he is quite taken aback by Jackson. In his diary, Steele writes, "General Jackson is famed for his hospitality, which is extended to all genteel strangers. I find that several of my friends who were opposed to him from principle, having visited his house, seem to forget the misconduct of the public officer in admiring him as a friend and citizen."

MARCH 4, 1829

Eight years after J. D. Steele's visit to the Hermitage, Andrew Jackson is inaugurated as the seventh president of the United States. "No one who was at Washington at the time...is likely to forget that period to the day of his death," writes a Jackson admirer of the festivities. The noise "still resounds in my ears," exclaims another eyewitness as Jackson steps onto the Capitol platform for the ceremony. Afterwards, a White House reception and a ball tops off what may go on record as the most flamboyant inauguration in American history.

MARCH 5, 1821

Several doctors meet to form the Medical Society of Nashville. Among the physicians attending the organizational session are Nashville's first-born son, Felix Robertson; A. G. Goodlett, future author of a widely acclaimed book on medicine; and Boyd McNairy. Robertson is elected president. Among other issues, it is decided for all present to "mutually pledge ourselves to the other under sanction of a solemn...promise."

MARCH 6, 1885

Following Samuel Watkins's gift of $100,000 and a free lot at the corner of Sixth Avenue, North and Church Street, residents gather to watch the dedication ceremonies for the city's first free school for the poor. Appropriately called Watkins Institute, the school will neither charge tuition, nor rely on taxes.

Samuel Watkins.

MARCH 7, 1905

The Southern Turf Saloon, a fashionable gentlemen's hangout on Fourth Avenue, North, between Union and Church Streets, is raided by Nashville Police for gambling activities. No one is arrested.

MARCH 8, 1859

Famed actor, Edwin Booth, brother of the future assassin of President Abraham Lincoln, opens a two weeks' engagement at the Gaiety Theater in Nashville. Booth's performances as Richard III packs the theater with record numbers.

MARCH 9, 1891

An unusually wet spring causes the Cumberland River to overflow its banks, resulting in considerable flood damage along the way.

MARCH 10, 1890

City government officials extend the Nashville town limits. Now, one hundred and ten years after the founding, Nashville stretches outward from the Public Square for two miles in all directions.

MARCH 11, 1819

Hundreds of wide-eyed residents gather as the *General Jackson*, a luxurious steamboat built at Pittsburgh at a cost of $16,000, docks at Nashville's wharf on lower Broad Street. It is the first instance in which a steamboat has made it all the way up the Cumberland River as far as Nashville. And, due to the tricky waters at the mouth of the Harpeth River, it will be two more years before the *General Jackson* makes another attempt. Nashville citizens, concerned that their town might be passed over by the rapidly developing steamboat traffic on the Cumberland, petition the state legislature to "make a law with provisions...permitting steamboats to pass to Nashville at all seasons of the year."

MARCH 12, 1780

The John Donelson party, on its way down the Tennessee River to rendezvous with James Robertson at the site of Nashville, approaches the fast water at Muscle Shoals. After considerable effort, the several flatboats in Donelson's small flotilla successfully shoot the rapids. A relieved Donelson writes in his diary that "by the hand of Providence, we are now preserved from this danger also."

MARCH 13, 1905

Senator William B. Bate, renowned Confederate general from neighboring Sumner County, is buried at Mount Olivet Cemetery in Nashville.

MARCH 14, 1933

Fifteen hundred homes are destroyed--half of them to the point of being uninhabitable--as a killer tornado sweeps through East Nashville. Lightning and downed power lines start many fires in the area, and when the destruction is over, scores of square blocks of homes along Woodland and Fatherland Streets, all the way out to Porter Road and Shelby Park, are demolished. More than three million dollars worth of damages in this lean Depression year make the East Nashville tornado one of the most damaging storms in the city's history.

MARCH 15, 1846

As nearly two thousand Nashvillians gather at the Presbyterian Church to witness the funeral of one of the town's leading citizens, Robert Porterfield, the victim's accused murderer sits

A COMPANY of Gentlemen of *North Carolina* having, for a large and valuable Confideration, purchafed from the Chiefs of the *Cherokee Indians*, by and with the Confent of the whole Nation, a confiderable Tract of their Lands, now called *Tranfylvania*, lying on the Rivers *Ohio*, *Cumberland*, and *Louifa*; and underftanding that many People are defirous of becoming Adventurers in that Part of the World, and wifh to know the Terms on which Lands in that Country may be had, they therefore hereby inform the Public, that any Perfon who will fettle on and inhabit the fame before the firft Day of *June* 1776, fhall have the Privilege of taking up and furveying for himfelf 500 Acres, and for each tithable Perfon he may carry with him and fettle there 250 Acres, on the Payment of 50 s. Sterling *per* Hundred, fubject to an yearly Quitrent of 2 s. like Money, to commence in the Year 1780. Such Perfons as are willing to become Purchafers may correfpond and treat with Mr. *William Johnfton* in *Hillfborough*, and Col. *John Williams* of *Granville*, *North Carolina*, or Col. *Richard Henderfon* at *Boonfborough*, in *Tranfylvania*.——This Country lies on the fouth Side of the Rivers *Ohio* and *Louifa*, in a temperate and healthy Climate. It is in general well watered with Springs and Rivulets, and has feveral Rivers, up which Veffels of confiderable Burthen may come with Eafe. In different Places of it are a Number of Salt Springs' where the making of Salt has been tried with great Succefs, and where, with Certainty, any Quantity needed may be eafily and conveniently made. Large Tracts of the Land lie on Lime-ftone, and in feveral Places there is Abundance of Iron Ore. The Fertility of the Soil, and Goodnefs of the Range, almoft furpafs Belief; and it is at prefent well ftored with Buffalo, Elk, Deer, Bear, Beaver, &c. and the Rivers abound with Fifh of various Kinds. Vaft Crowds of people are daily flocking to it, and many Gentlemen of the firft Rank and Character have bargained for Lands in it; fo that there is a great Appearance of a rapid Settlement, and that it will foon become a confiderable Colony, and one of the moft agreeable Countries in *America*.   (6)

Richard Henderson's land notice advertising for potential settlers in present-day Middle Tennessee.

dejectedly in the city jail. The prisoner--dime novelist Ned Buntline, who nearly a quarter of a century later will make "Buffalo Bill" Cody a household name across America--had escaped the night before from being killed himself by Porterfield's angry relatives. The mob had tried to lynch him, but he had escaped by leaping out the third story window of the City Hotel. Captured again, Buntline is finally released after pleading self-defense. He makes a hasty departure from Nashville.

MARCH 16, 1974

President Richard M. Nixon entertains millions of Americans on national television when he plays the piano and instructs Roy Acuff on how to use a yo-yo at the dedication of the new Grand Ole Opry House at Opryland, USA theme park.

MARCH 17, 1775

Entrepreneur Richard Henderson purchases large portions of Kentucky and Middle Tennessee from the Cherokee Indians during a treaty at Sycamore Shoals on the Watauga River. The purchase price for the twenty million acre parcel is two thousand pounds sterling and eight thousand pounds worth of trade goods. Henderson later becomes the organizer of the Robertson-Donelson parties that settle the site of Nashville on land bought from the Cherokees.

MARCH 18, 1903

David Lipscomb, a Church of Christ minister and co-founder of the Nashville Bible School, donates sixty-five acres of farmland on Granny White Pike to the school. When Lipscomb dies in 1918, the establishment becomes David Lipscomb College.

The Tennessee State Capitol Building, designed by Philadelphia architect, William Strickland.

MARCH 19, 1859

Fifteen years after the State Capitol was begun, the last stone on its terrace is put in place. William Strickland, the Capitol's renowned architect, was entombed in the building's north portico upon his death in 1854. Strickland's son directed the Capitol's completion.

MARCH 20, 1917

Nashvillians read in their newspapers that President Woodrow Wilson's cabinet advises him to declare war on Germany. Wilson had visited Nashville in 1905, when he was president of Princeton University. His brother, Joseph, was a one-time editor of the *Nashville Banner*, and his son-in-law, William Gibbs McAdoo, was a Tennessean by birth.

MARCH 21, 1850

Forty-three year old, Nashville-born Peter Hardeman Burnett, is sworn in as California's first elected American governor. Another Tennessean, Sumner Countian William McKendree Gwin, becomes one of the new state's two United States senators.

Charred remains of buildings destroyed in the East Nashville fire of March 22, 1916.

MARCH 22, 1916

A disastrous fire, started near the corner of North First and Oldham Streets by a child playing with a ball of burning yarn, destroys 648 buildings and displaces three thousand residents in a thirty-two square block area of East Nashville. Property damage estimated at two million dollars results from the inferno, described as "the most awe-inspiring spectacle ever witnessed in Nashville."

MARCH 23, 1747

Timothy Demonbreun, a Frenchman who lived in a cave high above the Cumberland River for several years before the first settlers arrived at the site of Nashville, is born in Canada. Demonbreun later lives in Nashville until his ninety-sixth year, when he dies and is buried in the old City Cemetery. Downtown's Demonbreun Street is named in his honor.

MARCH 24, 1864

General Nathan Bedford Forrest, born in neighboring Bedford County and a frequent and well-known visitor to Nashville, captures Union City, Tennessee, from Union forces.

General Nathan Bedford Forrest, the "Wizard of the Saddle," ranks among the most brilliant cavalry commanders the world has ever seen.

MARCH 25, 1909

Several Nashville women's clubs ask the City Council to restore the old, original names to the city's numbered streets. They suggest that First through Eighth Avenues be renamed Water, Market, College, Cherry, Summer, High, Vine, and Spruce Streets respectively. Their request is denied.

MARCH 26, 1873

Vanderbilt University becomes a practical reality when a half-million dollar bequest from Commodore Cornelius Vanderbilt is accepted by the Board of Trustees of Central University.

An early View of Vanderbilt University, pictured several years after its founding, sits atop Litton Hill off West End Avenue.

Solicited by Bishop Holland McTyeire, Vanderbilt's gift is eventually increased to one million dollars. A site, situated on Litton Hill west of town, is selected and construction begins the following year.

MARCH 27, 1814

General Andrew Jackson and a contingent of Tennessee militia defeat a large Creek Indian army at Horseshoe Bend in Alabama. Twenty-year old Sam Houston is severely wounded in the battle, and his persistence in continuing to fight despite his disabilities earns him the respect of Jackson. Shortly after the battle, the Creek chief, William Weatherford, sues for peace.

Sam Houston, having a barbed arrow removed forcefully from his thigh, at the battle of Horseshoe Bend

MARCH 28, 1900

The brilliant American actor, Richard Mansfield, plays Cyrano de Bergerac to a packed crowd at Nashville's thirteen year old Vendome Theater on Church Street. His portrayal draws a standing ovation.

MARCH 29, 1867

The first story ever printed about the recently organized Ku Klux Klan is published in a newspaper in Pulaski, Tennessee, the place of the organization's birth.

The Ku Klux Klan was founded in Pulaski, Tennessee in late 1866.

MARCH 30, 1907

The eminent black educator, Booker T. Washington, speaks to a gathering of theology students at Vanderbilt University.

MARCH 31, 1851

Nashville's Adelphi Theater, boasting the second largest stage in the United States, turns away hundreds of patrons who come to hear Jenny Lind, known as the "Swedish Nightingale." Lind's discoverer, the famed showman, P. T. Barnum, auctions available tickets to the concert, grossing eight thousand dollars for the first show alone.

APRIL 1, 1783

The Committee of Notables at Fort Nashborough establishes rules for the regulation of foreign whiskey sales in the settlement. One of the requirements calls for "any person bringing liquors here from foreign parts, shall, before they expose the same to sale, enter into bond with two sufficient securities, in the sum of two hundred pounds that they will not ask, take, or receive, directly or indirectly, any more than one silver dollar, or the value thereof in produce, for one quart of good, sound liquor."

The Battle of the Bluffs, in which Charlotte Robertson saved the day by releasing Fort Nashborough's dogs upon the Indians.

APRIL 2, 1781

After a band of marauding Indians lures James Robertson and about twenty of Fort Nashborough's defenders outside the stockade and into an ambush, Robertson's wife, Charlotte, takes matters into her own hands. Inside the fort is a pack of huge dogs used by the men to hunt bears. When the canines hear the commotion outside and start growling and howling, Mrs. Robertson opens the gates and lets them loose. The dogs

The giant balloon, Carnival, draws curious onlookers to Nashville's Public Square.

head straight for the fracas, causing great consternation among the terrified Indians. During the confusion, the settlers make it back to the fort, but not without casualty. Three men are killed in what becomes known as the "Battle of the Bluffs." Charlotte Robertson is sometimes called "savior of Nashville," for her quick action.

APRIL 3, 1877

Hundreds of wide-eyed Nashvillians watch in amazement as Professor Samuel A. King and Dr. A. C. Ford ascend from the Public Square in their hot-air balloon, called the *Carnival.* Several weeks later King and Ford again soar over Nashville in the basket of the *Buffalo*, the largest balloon in America. This time they glide to Gallatin, carrying mail from Nashville with them.

APRIL 4, 1891

Henry M. Stanley, the famed journalist who "found" the "lost" African missionary, Dr. David Livingston, lectures at Nashville's Vendome Theater. Stanley is on a national speaking tour and pulls into town aboard a private Pullman car decorated with his name on the side.

APRIL 5, 1865

William Gannaway Brownlow, a former East Tennessee Union-sympathizing circuit rider, assumes the office of governor of the State. Brownlow is despised by a large number of Tennesseans, particularly since they know he won the governor's race in a rigged election that prohibited disenfranchised Tennesseans from voting. The results of the election show that Brownlow receives 23,352 votes, while his opponent garners only 37.

William Gannaway "Parson" Brownlow.

Thousands of Nashvillians cheer returning heroes from the Great War in Europe.

APRIL 6, 1919

A quarter of a million people line the streets between downtown Nashville and Centennial Park to celebrate the end of the World War and the return home of American troops. The gathering is especially poignant for Tennesseans since the 30th Infantry Division, comprised mostly of soldiers from the Volunteer State, contributed prominently to the Allied victory over Germany when its soldiers broke through the Hindenburg Line in September, 1918.

APRIL 7, 1831

John H. Eaton, a former resident of Franklin and lately the secretary of war in Andrew Jackson's administration, resigns his post because of hostility shown toward Mrs. Eaton by Vice-president John C. Calhoun and other cabinet members.

John Overton's home, Traveller's Rest, shown during the War Between the States when it was used as a command post by General John Bell Hood.

APRIL 8, 1904

The Nashville Teachers' Association is organized, drawing together in a professional organization for the first time, school teachers from the area.

APRIL 9, 1766

John Overton--builder of Traveller's Rest, Andrew Jackson's law partner and campaign manager, Tennessee superior court judge, and one-time Supervisor of Federal Excise in President George Washington's administration--is born in Virginia.

Testing the strength of the Woodland Street Bridge.

APRIL 10, 1886

The new Woodland Street Bridge across the Cumberland River at the Public Square is checked for safety by subjecting each span to 400,000 pounds weight for ten minutes. The 639 foot long edifice passes the test with flying colors as a "steam roller, five fire engines, six hose carts, one hook and ladder, together with men and horses, also 32 wagons and 14 carts loaded with broken stone" parade across the bridge.

APRIL 11, 1898

The original St. Thomas Hospital, the brainchild of Bishop T. S. Byrne, opens its doors for business in the recently purchased Jacob McGavock Dickinson house, located between Hayes and Church Streets in Nashville's rapidly growing West End section. The first patient is the wife of a Baptist preacher.

APRIL 12, 1861

Confederate artillery under the command of General P. G. T. Beauregard opens fire on the Union arsenal at Fort Sumter, South Carolina. The War Between the States officially begins.

APRIL 13, 1856

A devastating fire strikes downtown Nashville. Supposedly started around 8:00 A.M. in the laundry room of the Nashville Inn, the flames quickly spread until they destroy the court house and half of the north side of the Public Square. Governor Andrew Johnson, who is staying at the Inn, loses twelve hundred dollars in the fire, while "gallantly assisting a lady."

APRIL 14, 1865

John Wilkes Booth, an actor who had just performed in Nashville the previous February, shoots President Abraham Lincoln in the back of the head while the Lincolns attend a play at Ford's Theater in Washington.

APRIL 15, 1865

Abraham Lincoln dies from the gunshot wound inflicted upon him the previous day by John Wilkes Booth. Vice-president Andrew Johnson, a former governor and military governor of Tennessee with offices in Nashville, assumes the presidency.

APRIL 16, 1829

Sam Houston, after a short, stormy marriage to Eliza Allen of Gallatin, resigns as Tennessee governor. General William Hall, the speaker of the Tennessee Senate and a renowned Indian fighter from Sumner County, becomes governor.

APRIL 17, 1919

Governor A. H. Roberts signs legislation that gives Tennessee women the right to vote for the first time in the State's history. The following year, Tennessee becomes the thirty-sixth and final state to ratify the Equal Suffrage Amendment, thus making it part of the U. S. Constitution.

APRIL 18, 1810

Alexander Wilson, a renowned painter of birds whose brilliant renditions preceded those of Audubon by at least twenty-five years, spends the night at Isaac Walton's farm and hostelry near Goodlettsville. While in the area, Wilson discovers and names two species of birds previously unknown to science, the Tennessee and the Nashville Warblers.

Alexander Wilson, the eminent painter.

APRIL 19, 1784

The official name of the tiny town on the bluffs high above the Cumberland River is changed from Fort Nashborough to Nashville.

APRIL 20, 1906

Charitable Nashvillians collect and send a train car full of food and clothes to the victims of the recent San Francisco earthquake.

APRIL 21, 1836

Former Nashvillian and Tennessee governor, Sam Houston, and a handful of dedicated Texans decisively defeat a large Mexican army under the command of President Santa Anna near the San Jacinto River. Santa Anna, himself, is captured, thus assuring the independence of Texas.

APRIL 22, 1898

The American Navy closes all Cuban ports, and the gunboat, *Nashville*, fires the first shot of the Spanish-American War. The *Nashville's* victim is the Spanish ship, *Buena Ventura*.

APRIL 23, 1907

Vanderbilt University initiates its program of spring football practice, beginning a tradition that succeeded in making the school's team one of the South's best for many years.

The arrival at Fort Nashborough of John Donelson's river party.

APRIL 24, 1780

John Donelson and his party of women and children arrive at Fort Nashborough after a torturous river journey from Fort Patrick Henry in what is now East Tennessee. The rendezvous of Donelson's group with the one that James Robertson brought to the bluffs the previous December marks the official beginning of Nashville.

APRIL 25, 1861

Governor Isham Harris calls a special session of the Tennessee Legislature to consider the "alarming and dangerous usurpation of power by the President." The week before, Harris had told the U. S. secretary of war that "Tennessee will not furnish a single man for purposes of coercion, but 50,000 if necessary for the defense of our rights and those of our Southern brothers."

APRIL 26, 1898

Congress officially declares war on Spain. Two newly-formed batteries of artillery drill on Nashville's Capitol Hill. One hundred and five days later, the war is over, and several Tennessee volunteer regiments never get to leave the United States.

APRIL 27, 1842

Former president of the United States, Martin Van Buren, arrives in Nashville aboard the steamboat, *Nashville*. During Van Buren's month-long stay in the city, he visits his old friend, Andrew Jackson, on numerous occasions.

APRIL 28, 1897

A preview of the upcoming Centennial Exposition is held for Nashvillians. Ten thousand lights are used in a glorious display that will highlight the activities celebrating Tennessee's one hundredth anniversary as a state. Because of the grandiose plans for the occasion, however, the festivities are one year late.

APRIL 29, 1903

The noted musician, Victor Herbert, and fifty of his associates perform at Nashville's Tabernacle.

APRIL 30, 1889

Nashville's first electric street car is put into operation on a route that runs from downtown out West End Avenue to the vicinity of today's Centennial Park.

MAY 1, 1940

The Belle Meade Theater on Harding Road is opened to the public. E. L. Jordan, the theater's manager, starts a tradition called the "Wall of Fame," whereby visiting illuminaries autograph the wall. The Hollywood actress, Irene Dunn, is the first person to sign her name to the wall, and over the next several decades she is followed by such notables as Charlton Heston, Andy Griffith, Gene Autry, Maureen O'Hara, Doris Day, Perry Como, Bob Hope, and Walt Disney.

MAY 2, 1978

Miss Mary Northern, an elderly East Nashville recluse who has made national headlines after she was forcibly removed from her Gallatin Road home by city officials, dies. Northern is remembered for her fight which epitomized the individual's right to self-determination when she refused to have her gangrenous feet amputated in order to spare her life.

Opening day at the Tennessee Centennial Celebration.

MAY 3, 1897

Just in time for the beginning of festivities on June 1, the Woman's Building at the Tennessee Centennial exhibition is officially opened to the public.

MAY 4, 1825

The Marquis de Lafayette, General Lafayette of Revolutionary War fame, visits Nashville as part of his national tour. The occasion is called "one of the greatest social events in the history of Nashville." Received by General A n d r e w Jackson and a committee of city fathers,

General Lafayette, who had greatly assisted in the American war effort against Great Britain during the Revolution.

Lafayette is welcomed by twenty thousand people as he surveys the city in a carriage drawn by four white horses.

MAY 5, 1979

After gracing the corner of Fourth Avenue and Church Street for more than one hundred years, the Maxwell House Hotel moves to its new location in Metro Center. At its old site on the corner of Fourth Avenue and Church Street, where it was destroyed by fire in 1961, the famous hotel had hosted seven American presidents.

MAY 6, 1861

The Tennessee Legislature votes to take Tennessee out of the Union, subject to a public referendum to be held on June 8.

MAY 7, 1890

George Jordan, a freed slave from Williamson County who joined the United States Army in Nashville shortly after the end of the War Between the States, is awarded the Medal of Honor for gallant service at Fort Tularosa and Carrizo Canyon, New Mexico, in 1880 and 1881, during the Apache Wars. According to the official citation, Jordan, a member of the famous all-black Buffalo Soldiers, "stubbornly held his ground in an extremely exposed position and gallantly forced back a much superior number of the enemy, preventing them from surrounding the command."

Sergeant George Jordan, Williamson County's contribution to the famed "Buffalo Soldiers."

MAY 8, 1824

William Walker, who in his short life will become known all over the Western Hemisphere as the "gray-eyed man of destiny" because of his filibustering exploits in Central America, is born on High Street (now Sixth Avenue).

MAY 9, 1857

The American Medical Association holds its annual meeting in Nashville. Nashvillian, Dr. Paul Eve, is elected as the organization's president.

MAY 10, 1910

Donau, a two-year old owned by the Gerst family of Nashville, wins the thirty-sixth "Running of the Roses." In walking away with the Kentucky Derby, Donau earns for his masters $4,850, running the course in 2:06 2/5, just short of an all-time record.

MAY 11, 1906

Former Governor Robert L. Taylor defeats Nashville newspaperman Edward Ward Carmack in the Democratic primary race for United States senator. Taylor goes on to win the senate seat in the fall general election.

MAY 12, 1907

The *Nashville Tennesse* an begins publication as Nashville's morning newspaper.

MAY 13, 1797

The Duke of Orleans, Louis Philippe, who thirty-three years later will be crowned king of France, leaves Nashville after a four-day visit. Of his tour in the infant town, the Duke later writes, "We lodged at Captain Maxwell's. We would have been comfortable enough there if court had not been in session; as it was, the house was full, and even sleeping on the floor there was hardly room." For eighteen years,

Louis Philippe visited Nashville several years before he was crowned King of France.

Louis Philippe ruled France as the "citizen king," and whenever Americans visited his court, he delighted in asking them if "they still sleep three in a bed in Tennessee?"

MAY 14, 1892

The noted revivalist, Sam Jones, opens a series of gospel meetings at the Tabernacle, now the Ryman Auditorium.

MAY 15, 1908

A local newspaper article reveals that there are five hundred automobile owners in Nashville.

MAY 16, 1771

The Battle of Alamance, credited with sending many of its defeated North Carolinians across the Appalachian Mountains

*The Battle of Alamance, referred to by some historians as the first battle of the
American Revolution.*

to Watauga and subsequently to the Cumberland River valley,
is fought. The conflict pits North Carolina colonials against
troops of the royal governor and occurs near the town of
Hillsborough, North Carolina.

MAY 17, 1909

Ground-breaking ceremonies for the Young Men's Christian
Association (YMCA) are held in a lot on the southeast corner
of Seventh Avenue, North and Union Street. A local chapter of
the "Y" was first organized in Nashville thirty-four years earlier, operating out of a building on Church Street for several
years. The building at Seventh and Union was razed in 1972 to
make room for a high-rise hotel.

MAY 18, 1938

The Natchez Trace Parkway, following an ancient Indian trail
and an historic commercial thoroughfare linking Natchez,

Mississippi with Nashville, becomes a unit in the United States National Park
Service.

The official emblem of the Natchez Trace Parkway.

MAY 19, 1906

Plans are announced to widen the Hillsboro Pike by ten feet on each side to provide room for streetcar tracks.

MAY 20, 1880

The equestrian statue of Andrew Jackson is unveiled on the State Capitol grounds. Before the day ends, some thirty-thousand people will gather for the ceremonies and a look at the bronze masterpiece by famed sculptor, Clark Mills. Only two replicas of the statue exist, one in Lafayette Park across Pennsylvania Avenue from the White House and one in Jackson Square in New Orleans.

Thousands watch at the unveiling of Andrew Jackson's statue on the State Capitol grounds.

MAY 21, 1890

For the second time in thirty-three years, the American Medical Association meets in Nashville. Eight hundred physicians from all over the United States gather at the Vendome Theater in what is called the "greatest medical exhibition" ever held outside of St. Louis. Since the first time the AMA met in the city in 1857, eight Nashvillians have been elected to its presidency: Paul Eve, William Bowling, William Briggs, John

A. Witherspoon, William Haggard, Jr., Harrison Shoulders, Olin West, and Thomas Nesbitt.

MAY 22, 1903

The new Arcade receives thousands of visitors on its third day of operation. The idea for the structure is the brainchild of a Nashvillian, Daniel Buntin, who studied the building style in Italy and organized a company in 1902, whose purpose was to build a commercial arcade in Nashville. The unique edifice runs for 360 feet between Fourth and Fifth Avenues, North, and is eighty feet wide. Designed to house two tiers of shops, fifty-two in all, the structure sprawls over nearly an acre.

MAY 23, 1835

Several hundred Nashville residents turn out at the Vauxhall Gardens to hear native-son John Bell endorse Knoxvillian Hugh Lawson White for the presidency of the United States over President Andrew Jackson's personal choice, Martin Van Buren. Although Van Buren wins the election, White carries Tennessee. Bell has no idea that he will someday run for president against a man of whom no one has ever heard--Abraham Lincoln.

MAY 24, 1864

A minor skirmish between Confederate and Union forces occurs near Nashville. Federal troops still occupy the capital city more than two years after its occupation. Nashville remains one of the best fortified and well-equipped enemy positions in the entire South.

MAY 25, 1903

Anticipating that the automobile is here to stay, the Nashville Auto Club is organized.

MAY 26, 1846

Shortly after the United States and Mexico go to war, Governor Aaron V. Brown issues a request for 2,800 Tennessee volunteers for military service; more than thirty thousand respond. From that time on, Tennessee has been called the "Volunteer State," renewing a name first conferred upon it during the War of 1812 when the same volunteer spirit prevailed in that conflict.

MAY 27, 1865

President Andrew Johnson, the former governor of Tennessee,

orders the release of most people who have been imprisoned in the South by the Union military establishment. Two days later, the President issues a proclamation that grants amnesty to large numbers of those who participated in "the existing rebellion."

President Andrew Johnson.

MAY 28, 1907

The statue of railroad magnate, Jere Baxter, is dedicated at Sixteenth Avenue and Broad Street. The statue is later moved to the front yard of Jere Baxter School in Inglewood.

Jere Baxter, founder of the Tennessee Central Railroad.

MAY 29, 1805

Former Vice-president Aaron Burr arrives in Nashville as a guest of Andrew Jackson.

Former Vice-president Aaron Burr

MAY 30, 1806

Because of a disparaging remark against his beloved wife, Rachel, Andrew Jackson kills the man who made the error in judgment, Nashvillian Charles Dickinson, in a duel just across the Kentucky state border.

MAY 31, 1897

The Tennessee Central Railroad, with headquarters in Nashville, is sold to St. Louis businessmen for $125,000.

JUNE 1, 1796

Although Nashvillians could not have known at the time, their small town on the bluffs above the Cumberland River is destined to become the capital of Tennessee as the former Territory of the United States South of the River Ohio becomes the sixteenth state on June 1, 1796. After a convention held at Knoxville in January, 1796, to determine the Territory's fate, the first legislature meets and John Sevier is elected the first governor.

John Sevier, first governor of the State of Tennessee.

JUNE 2, 1930

Charles Elder, a recent graduate of David Lipscomb College, opens his first bookstore on the ground floor of a building across Church Street from the Maxwell House Hotel. A year or so later, Elder moves his business to Fifth Avenue between Union Street and the Arcade. Over the years, Elder's establishment becomes one of the premier rare and out-of-print book-stores in the United States.

JUNE 3, 1978

Nashville native, George Sloan, becomes the first non-Briton to ever win the British Amateur Steeplechase.

JUNE 4, 1936

Robertson County native, Joseph Byrns, United States congressman who represented the Nashville district, and, of late, served as the Speaker of the U. S. House of Representatives, dies. President Franklin D. Roosevelt attends the funeral at Mount Olivet Cemetery.

JUNE 5, 1850

The Nashville Convention, which started on June 4, is in full swing. Delegates from nine Southern states attend the series of meetings to form a strong, dedicated Southern political party that will advocate the extension of slavery into California and the southwestern regions of the country recently acquired from Mexico. The Compromise of 1850, which admits California as a free state and extends to Utah and New Mexico territories the authority to allow slavery or not, more or less abrogates the guidelines formulated during the Nashville Convention.

JUNE 6, 1902

A "Last Days of Pompeii" fireworks display is viewed by thousands of Nashvillians at the new Centennial Park, which has replaced the exhibits used in the Tennessee Centennial celebration in 1897.

JUNE 7, 1905

The Nashville Retail Merchants' Association votes to sponsor the Tennessee State Fair without government financial assistance.

JUNE 8, 1861

Tennesseans again vote in a popular referendum over the issue of secession. Governor Isham Harris, on April 25, had strongly urged the Tennessee Legislature to endorse taking Tennessee out of the Union. Lawmakers agreed, subject to the June 8 vote. The results: 104,913 for secession; 47,238 against. Tennessee thus becomes the last of the Confederate states to secede.

Isham G. Harris, Tennessee's war-time governor.

JUNE 9, 1819

James Monroe, fifth president of the United States and the first chief executive to visit Nashville, arrives in town in the company of General Andrew Jackson who has traveled to Georgia to accompany the President to the Hermitage. Anticipating "women's lib" by 150 years, Monroe speaks to the lady students at the Nashville Female Academy. He says, "The female presents capacities for improvements, and has equal claims to it, with the other sex. Without intermitting our attention to the improvement of the one, let us extend it alike to the other."

Nashville Female Academy, located on the site of downtown Nashville's YMCA at Ninth Avenue and Church Street.

JUNE 10, 1845

Former President Andrew Jackson, who died on June 8, is laid to rest beside his beloved Rachel in the Hermitage gardens. One of the most powerful, yet controversial presidents the Nation has ever had, Jackson was sometimes sarcastically dubbed by his political opponents as "King Andrew."

JUNE 11, 1843

Nashville's "first lady," Charlotte Robertson, dies at the age of ninety-two. She is buried in the old City Cemetery on Oak Street in South Nashville.

Nashville's beloved Charlotte Reeves Robertson, wife of the town's founder.

JUNE 12, 1897

President and Mrs. William McKinley visit the Tennessee Centennial Exposition, located at present-day Centennial Park off West End Avenue. Six weeks earlier, from Washington, D. C., the President had, through the magic of electricity, opened the gates to the Exposition by pushing a button. Now, he and Mrs. McKinley leisurely stroll through the exhibit buildings observing all of the wonderful collections assembled there.

JUNE 13, 1922

Murfreesboro writer, Mary Noilles Murfree, who in her youth attended the Nashville Female Academy and lived in a home at the corner of Ninth Avenue, South and Demonbreun Street, receives an honorary doctor of literature degree from the University of the South. In order to get published, Miss Murfree used the pen name of Charles Egbert Craddock, and for years, her editors thought she was a man.

Murfreesboro and Nashville writer Mary Noailles Murfree.

JUNE 14, 1864

Former Columbia resident, Lieutenant-general Leonidas Polk, is killed in action at Pine Mountain, Georgia.

JUNE 15, 1849

Former President James K. Polk dies at his home, Polk Place, in Nashville. Polk became the Nation's first "dark-horse"

Polk Place in Nashville, the last home of President James K. Polk.

presidential candidate when he was nominated on the eighth ballot at the 1844 Democratic National Convention. He was the only one-term president ever to fulfill all of his announced campaign promises. Polk survives the presidency only three months before he succumbs to complications from cholera.

JUNE 16, 1906

Officials of Vanderbilt University purchase the property upon which to build the school's football stadium. Upon completion, Dudley Field will seat more spectators than any other college stadium in the Southeast.

JUNE 17, 1861

The United States flag is lowered from the State Capitol building and replaced with the Confederate States' "Stars and Bars."

over eight months, the "Stars and Bars" will be pulled down and replaced with "Old Glory."

The Confederate "Stars and Bars."

JUNE 18, 1801

Mary Middleton Rutledge, the granddaughter of two signers of the Declaration of Independence, is born. Miss Rutledge later marries Francis Fogg, a Connecticut lawyer and educator, and the couple become leading citizens in Nashville.

JUNE 19, 1845

Final blueprints for the Tennessee State Capitol are approved by the Legislature. The winning plan is by eminent Philadelphia architect, William Strickland, and the building is designed to top Campbell's Hill, or, as it is sometimes called, Cedar Knob. The capitol's tower is copied after a unique design by *Lysicrates, the Athenian.*

William Strickland, designer of the Tennessee State Capitol.

JUNE 20, 1873

Seventy-two Nashvillians die of cholera within the twenty-four hour period. The epidemic has its beginnings at the State Prison, then located on Church Street at Fourteenth Avenue. The day goes down in history as "Black Friday."

The J. B. Richardson *(left), one of Captain Tom Ryman's steamboats, docked at the foot of Broad Street*

JUNE 21, 1904

The steamboat, *J. B. Richardson*, hits a snag at the mouth of the Harpeth River, the location of a dangerous shoal in the Cumberland River, but all of the craft's passengers and crew survive.

JUNE 22, 1904

James Robertson's old homeplace, located on the Charlotte Pike, is subdivided and sold at auction.

JUNE 23, 1863

U. S. General William Rosecrans and his army move on Tullahoma, Tennessee.

JUNE 24, 1936

American Airlines lands its first commercial airplane at Berry Field. The airport is named in honor of Colonel Harry S.

Berry Field, Nashville's commercial airport for many years prior to the opening of the new Nashville International.

Berry, who supervised its construction under the guidance of the Works Progress Administration. Three other facilities have previously served Nashville's air transportation needs: one located at Hampton Road and Woodmont Boulevard and used until 1921; Blackwood Field, located off Shute Lane near the Hermitage, used until 1928; and an airstrip that occupied today's McCabe Park.

JUNE 25, 1802

Three horse thieves are publicly hanged on Nashville's Public Square.

JUNE 26, 1903

The Nashville Railway and Light Company is organized in the office of J. C. Bradford. Percy Warner is elected the company's first president.

JUNE 27, 1908

Incumbent Governor Malcolm Patterson defeats Edward Ward Carmack in the Democratic primary for Tennessee governor.

JUNE 28, 1962

Nashville and Davidson County voters approve a resolution calling for consolidation of the two governments. The concept, already soundly defeated earlier, in 1958, calls for one "Metro" government with single services, taxes, schools, and leadership. Metropolitan Nashville is born. Ironically, Nashville's founder, James Robertson, was born on this day in 1742.

JUNE 29, 1905

Nashville's first garage specializing in automobile repairs is opened at the corner of Ninth Avenue, North and Church Street.

JUNE 30, 1863

The Confederate Army evacuates Tullahoma and withdraws across the Tennessee River. Nashville remains under Union occupation.

JULY 1, 1820

The Tennessee Historical Society has its beginnings when the Tennessee Antiquarian Society is organized by John Haywood, a noted jurist, historian, and writer.

Belmont, the home of Adelicia and Joseph Acklen,
one of the South's premier estates.

JULY 2, 1839

Adelicia Hayes, who in later life becomes mistress of the Belmont plantation, marries her first husband, Isaac Franklin, a fifty-year old planter from Gallatin. In 1849, the widowed Adelicia marries Joseph Acklen, a descendant of the family that founded Huntsville, Alabama. Finally, after Joseph dies, Adelicia is married a final time, to Dr. William Cheatham. During her lifetime, Adelicia Hayes Franklin Acklen Cheatham was considered one of the wealthiest women in America.

JULY 3, 1918

In the tiny village of Old Hickory, just a few miles from downtown Nashville, the E. I. Du Pont Company produces its first gunpowder to supply the Allied forces participating in the great war in Europe. The plant has a daily output of 700,000 pounds of powder, making it the largest such producer in the world.

JULY 4, 1892

The Capital City Cycling Club sponsors its one hundred mile event that takes scores of cyclists along the backroads of Middle Tennessee. The course goes from Nashville to Lebanon to Murfreesboro to Eagleville to Triune and back to Nashville. Most competitors complete the race in about eight and one-half hours.

Christ Episcopal Church at the corner of Ninth Avenue and Broad Street.

JULY 5, 1830

Episcopalian officials lay the cornerstone to Christ Church at the northeast corner of today's Sixth Avenue and Church Street. First services are held in the new building by George Weller about one year later. In 1887, the church moves its sanctuary to the corner of Ninth Avenue and Broad Street, where it remains today.

JULY 6, 1905

Fire destroys the Louisville and Nashville railroad shops.

JULY 7, 1797

Tennessee Senator William Blount, the former territorial governor, is impeached and expelled by the United States Congress for conspiracy to wage war on Spain. The Senate later drops the charges in this early instance of impeachment proceedings against an American governmental official. Blount is later elected to the Tennessee Senate and serves honorably until his death.

JULY 8, 1979

Sports journalist legend, Fred Russell, is honored at the Belle Meade Country Club for fifty years of service at the *Nashville Banner*.

JULY 9, 1918

In what has been termed the worst railroad tragedy in United States history, more than one hundred workers, predominantly black, are killed near White Bridge Road as two passenger trains of the Nashville, Chattanooga, and St. Louis Railroad line hit head-on.

JULY 10, 1805

A military court-martial finds Nashvillian Colonel Thomas Butler guilty of "mutinous conduct" for refusing to cut his hair.

JULY 11, 1804

Vice-president of the United States Aaron Burr, who will become a frequent visitor to Nashville, inflicts a mortal gunshot wound to former secretary of the treasury, Alexander Hamilton, in a duel.

JULY 12, 1856

William Walker, the "gray-eyed man of destiny," is inaugurated as president of Nicaragua, the high point of the Nashville soldier of fortune's career. Walker's success is short-lived, however. In less than five years, he will be executed by a Honduran firing squad.

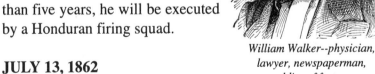

William Walker--physician, lawyer, newspaperman, soldier of fortune.

JULY 13, 1862

Nathan Bedford Forrest makes an attempt to free Middle Tennessee from Union occupation when he attacks and captures the Federal garrison at Murfreesboro.

JULY 14, 1894

With an eye on planning and implementing an indelible celebration to herald Tennessee's upcoming one hundredth birthday in 1896, the Centennial Exposition Company is chartered by the State in Nashville.

JULY 15, 1905

Duncan Dorris advertises the arrival of a number of brand new four-cylinder "St. Louis" automobiles at his garage at the corner of Ninth Avenue and Church Street.

JULY 16, 1889

The National Educational Association opens its thirty-second annual convention in Nashville.

JULY 17, 1862

President Abraham Lincoln signs the Second Confiscation Act that authorizes the United States government to free slaves in occupied territory, including the Nashville area.

JULY 18, 1830

John and Peggy Eaton, used to receiving the cold shoulder in Washington, D. C., arrive in

Margaret "Peggy" Eaton, wife of Franklin's John H. Eaton.

Nashville amidst a warm, hometown welcome. Eaton, a Franklin resident and President Andrew Jackson's secretary of war, and Peggy are criticized by Washington society for marrying so soon after Peggy's first husband was killed at sea.

JULY 19, 1901

The Nashville *Daily News* appears with Murfreesboro native, Grantland Rice, on the staff as writer. Rice will go on to become one of the Nation's most recognized names in sports reporting.

JULY 20, 1906

The Nashville Railway and Light Company buys a site on Charlotte Avenue, between Third and Fourth Avenues, for an extension of its transfer station.

JULY 21, 1821

Ralph E. W. Earle, a noted portrait painter who lived at the Hermitage for many years, digs into an Indian mound on the banks of the Cumberland River. Earle's careful and thoughtful excavation of the mound reveals that it is the one upon which the French trader, Charleville, built his post and store in 1710.

JULY 22, 1822

As the result of several revival meetings held on the site of today's Hume-Fogg School, the first Baptist church in Nashville is organized. Within a few short years, the Baptists will own the largest church building in the city, located on Church Street between Sixth and Seventh Avenues.

JULY 23, 1950

Less than a month after North Korean troops march south across the 38th Parallel on June 25, 1950, thirty-one Tennessee Air National Guardsmen from Nashville, en route home from summer camp, are killed in a plane crash near Myrtle Beach, South Carolina.

JULY 24, 1907

Typhoid runs rampant throughout the city. Hundreds of Nashville residents are ill as summer temperatures climb to one hundred degrees.

JULY 25, 1903

The Duncan Hotel, at the corner of Fourth Avenue and Charlotte Street, suffers $4,000 worth of fire damage, as three Nashville firemen are hurt.

JULY 26, 1907

Scores of Nashvillians brave the intense summer heat to watch ground breaking ceremonies for Cathedral Catholic Church on West End Avenue, where it remains standing today.

JULY 27, 1952

As Nashvillians experience one of the city's hottest Julys on record, the mercury climbs to 107.3 degrees, the highest temperature ever registered locally.

JULY 28, 1901

Nashville businessman, Jere Baxter, makes a speech requesting the public's support of the railroad bond issue in the upcoming referendum.

The old Duncan Hotel which once stood on the corner of present-day Fourth Avenue and Charlotte Street.

One of Nashville's earlier airports, Blackwood Field.

JULY 29, 1924

Regular air mail postal service begins in Nashville at Blackwood Field near the Hermitage. A small plane carrying letters and packages departs for Chicago, arriving there three hours and twenty-nine minutes later.

JULY 30, 1887

Harper's Weekly devotes a two-page spread, complete with illustrations, to deer hunting at Belle Meade Plantation. The article reads, "Belle Meade, which is one of the largest, oldest, and most reliable horse breeding establishments in the world, is situated on the Harding or Richland Pike, about six miles out of Nashville. It embraces 5,300 acres of Blue Grass land, watered by rippling brooks, and shaded in many parts by the indigenous oaks and hickories of this part of the country; and a stone wall, twenty-two miles long...."

JULY 31, 1797

Francis Baily, who later will become the founder and four-time president of the Royal Astronomical Society in England, approaches Nashville from the south on his overland journey

Belle Meade, the "queen" of Southern plantations.

from Natchez. Arriving at the residence of a Mr. Jocelyn--namesake for today's Jocelyn Hollow Road--Baily remarks in his journal that the farm "consisted of several acres of land tolerably well cultivated; some in corn, some in meadow, and others in grain." The hungry Englishman is fed boiled bacon, French beans, and cornbread.

Title-page from Francis Baily's book documenting his American travels, including his trip up the Natchez Trace to Nashville.

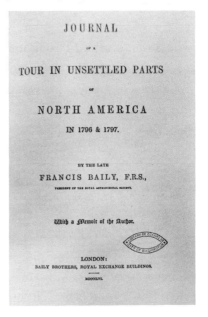

JOURNAL

OF A

TOUR IN UNSETTLED PARTS

OF

NORTH AMERICA

IN 1796 & 1797.

BY THE LATE

FRANCIS BAILY, F.R.S.,

PRESIDENT OF THE ROYAL ASTRONOMICAL SOCIETY.

With a Memoir of the Author.

LONDON:
BAILY BROTHERS, ROYAL EXCHANGE BUILDINGS.

MDCCCLVI.

AUGUST 1, 1787

James Robertson, founder of Nashville.

James Robertson notifies State of Franklin Governor John Sevier the he fears an attack on the Cumberland settlements by Indians. Robertson writes, "We are informed that at a grand council held by the Creeks, it was determined, by that whole nation, to their utmost this fall to cut off this country...the people are drawing together in large stations, and doing everything necessary for their defence. But, I fear, without some timely assistance, we shall chiefly fall a sacrafice...."

AUGUST 2, 1897

The internationally acclaimed, Irish-born composer of light opera, Victor Herbert, along with his Thirty-second Regiment Band of New York, arrives in Nashville for a thirty-eight day engagement at the Tennessee Centennial Exposition. Herbert becomes a regular patron of the Southern Turf, a well-respected gentlemen's saloon located on Fourth Avenue, North. While passing time at the Southern Turf, Herbert pens part of his opera, *The Fortune Teller*.

AUGUST 3, 1958

Tennessee naval Commander William R. Anderson navigates the nuclear submarine, *Nautilus*, under the North Pole.

AUGUST 4, 1907

Vanderbilt's football stadium, to be called Dudley Field, is begun as funds slowly become available.

AUGUST 5, 1946

The first natural gas for home consumption arrives in Nashville from Texas through large underground pipes. This new convenience is a far cry from the first manufactured gas produced by the Nashville Gas Light Company in 1850 and used by city officials for street lamps, and, years later, for residential stoves.

AUGUST 6, 1896

The American Protective Association candidate for Davidson County sheriff beats the Democratic Party choice by six votes.

AUGUST 7, 1960

The Shelby Street Bridge across the Cumberland River, also called the Sparkman Street Bridge, is closed for repairs.

AUGUST 8, 1901

A public referendum approves a bond issue which allows for the formation of the reorganized Tennessee Central Railroad.

AUGUST 9, 1920

The Nineteenth Amendment (Women's Suffrage) is considered by the Tennessee Legislature in a special session.

AUGUST 10, 1892

Nashville civic leader, Douglas Anderson, reveals to the news media his idea for a magnificent Tennessee Centennial Exposition to commemorate the one hundredth anniversary of Tennessee's admission into the Union.

AUGUST 11, 1893

The nation-wide "financial panic" of 1893 hits Nashville. The Fourth National Bank opens its doors as usual, but by 11:15 A. M., so much cash has been paid out that managers instruct the tellers to honor requests for only one hundred dollars or less.

AUGUST 12, 1862

Confederate Colonel John Hunt Morgan and his elite 2d Kentucky Cavalry sweep into Gallatin and capture the Union garrison there. The raid is part of a devastating three-week campaign into Tennessee and Kentucky and prompts President Abraham Lincoln to wire the Union general in command of the region, "They are having a stampede in Kentucky. Please look to it."

John Hunt Morgan, the Confederate

AUGUST 13, 1966

The Metropolitan Nashville Historical Commission is founded.

AUGUST 14, 1891

Mrs. James K. Polk, the former Sarah Childress of Murfreesboro, dies at Polk Place in Nashville just twenty-one days short of her eighty-eighth birthday. She has survived her husband by forty-two years. Tennessee Governor John Price Buchanan writes, " She has stood a peer among the women of the land, a perfect type of the gentle womanhood of the old South, and her influence will live forever."

Mrs. James Knox Polk, the first lady of Nashville for many years after her husband's death.

AUGUST 15, 1939

The Tennessee Valley Authority (TVA), a federally-funded program organized during the early days of President Franklin D. Roosevelt's adminstration, purchases the Tennessee Electric Power Company.

AUGUST 16, 1977

Elvis Presley, the "king" of rock and roll and a frequent visitor to Nashville's recording studios, dies in Memphis.

Elvis Presley was one of the first American musicians to be honored by a postage stamp.

AUGUST 17, 1905

Plans for the construction of a new building on the Vanderbilt University campus, to be known as Furman Hall, are approved by the Furman family.

The U. S. Customs House, still standing,
that was so long coming to Nashville.

AUGUST 18, 1856

Federal officials promise Nashvillians a customs house. Almost seventeen years later, Congress finally authorizes the structure, to be located at the corner of Seventh Avenue and Broad Street. The building will be built "for the use and accommodation of the courts of the United States, the post office, custom house, and other offices of the Government, at a cost...not exceeding the sum of $150,000." President Rutherford B. Hayes lays the cornerstone on September 19, 1877. The building remains standing and in use today.

AUGUST 19, 1862

Union troops begin a series of raids on the Louisville and Nashville Railroad in East Nashville and in Sumner County

AUGUST 20, 1852

Nashville newspaper editor, Felix Zollicoffer, duels with John Marling. Neither man is seriously injured.

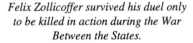
Felix Zollicoffer survived his duel only to be killed in action during the War Between the States.

AUGUST 21, 1895

West Side Race Track, the site of today's Centennial Park, is selected as the location for the upcoming Tennessee Centennial Exposition.

AUGUST 22, 1800

William Selby Harney, who will later serve his country's military establishment over a period of seven decades, is born at Haysborough, near today's Spring Hill Cemetery.

General William Selby Harney was called "The Hornet" by his Teton Sioux foes because of his relentless pursuit of them during the Plains Indian wars of the 1850s.

AUGUST 23, 1861

Governor Isham Harris pleads with Nashville mothers, wives, and daughters of soldiers to provide the Confederate Army with clothing and blankets.

AUGUST 24, 1889

Nashville's reservoir, located on a high hill overlooking Eighth Avenue, South, is completed.

AUGUST 25, 1960

The Olympic games open in Rome, Italy. Before the competition

Wilma Rudolph and a photo of the 1956 A & I women's Olympic team, with Coach Ed Temple in the middle

is over, Clarksville native, Wilma Rudolph, and Ralph Boston, both students at Tennessee Agricultural and Industrial College (today's Tennessee State University) bring home the gold. Rudolph takes gold medals for the 100 meter, 200 meter, and women's relay events. Boston wins gold for the men's long jump competition.

AUGUST 26, 1852

The Nashville City Council supports financial backing for the city's public school system.

AUGUST 27, 1909

Nashville's first police raid operating under the new prohibition laws closes a Greek restaurant on Broad Street.

AUGUST 28, 1802

French naturalist, Francois Andre Michaux, arrives in Nashville. He describes the settlement as "the principal and oldest town in this part of Tennessee...situated upon the river Cumberland." Although impressed by the prosperity of Nashville's residents as compared to other areas he has visited, he finds that the town "contains no kind of manufactory or public establishment."

AUGUST 29, 1925

The Andrew Jackson Hotel, located on the site of today's Tennessee Performing Arts Center, opens for business. Like other fine hostelries in the city--the Maxwell House, St. Cloud, Hermitage, Duncan, and Tulane--the Andrew Jackson soon becomes noted for its fine food, good accommodations, and friendly service.

TRAVELS

TO THE WEST OF THE

ALLEGHANY MOUNTAINS,

IN THE STATES OF

𝕺𝖍𝖎𝖔,

KENTUCKY, AND TENNESSEA,

AND BACK TO CHARLESTON, BY THE UPPER CAROLINES;

COMPRISING

The most interesting Details on the present State of

𝕬𝖌𝖗𝖎𝖈𝖚𝖑𝖙𝖚𝖗𝖊,

AND

THE NATURAL PRODUCE OF THOSE COUNTRIES:

TOGETHER WITH

Particulars relative to the Commerce that exists between the above-mentioned States, and those situated East of the Mountains and Low Louisiana,

UNDERTAKEN, IN THE YEAR 1802,

UNDER THE AUSPICES OF

His Excellency M. CHAPTAL, Minister of the Interior,

BY F. A. MICHAUX,

MEMBER OF THE SOCIETY OF NATURAL HISTORY AT PARIS; CORRES-PONDENT OF THE AGRICULTURAL SOCIETY IN THE DEPARTMENT OF THE SEINE AND OISE.

𝕷𝖔𝖓𝖉𝖔𝖓:

Printed by D. N. SHURY, Berwick Street, Soho;

FOR B. CROSBY AND CO. STATIONERS' COURT;

AND J. F. HUGHES, WIGMORE STREET, CAVENDISH SQUARE.

1805.

Title-page of F. A. Michaux's book about his travels to America, including his trip to Nashville and vicinity in 1802.

AUGUST 30, 1881

For bravery in the line of duty on this day during the Apache Wars in Arizona Territory, First-lieutenant William H. Carter, 6th United States Cavalry, is awarded the Medal of Honor on September 17, 1891. The Nashvillian is cited for rescuing wounded soldiers from under heavy fire.

AUGUST 31, 1875

Jesse James, Jr. is born on Boscobel Street in Edgefield. His infamous father, Jesse, is living there under the alias, J. D. Howard. The elder James presents himself to his unsuspecting neighbors as a grain dealer and a lover of fine horses. Sometimes he plays cards with the local police. Jesse's equally infamous brother, Frank, lives down the street under the alias, Ben J. Woodson.

$25,000 REWARD

JESSE JAMES

DEAD OR ALIVE

$15,000 REWARD FOR FRANK JAMES

$5000 Reward for any Known Member of the James Band

SIGNED:
ST. LOUIS MIDLAND RAILROAD

Frank and Jesse James were already wanted men when Jesse's son was born in Edgefield (East Nashville). An old reward poster.

SEPTEMBER 1, 1877

In an experiment that amazes Nashville residents, Mrs. James K. Polk, widow of the eleventh president of the United States, talks over the telephone to Mr. A. G. Adams. After Mrs. Polk's premier use of this astonishing new device, Dr. James Ross installs the first phone in the city, connecting his residence on Fifth Avenue with his office on the Public Square. Telephone service costs five dollars a month, and by 1884, more than six hundred residences sport one of the instruments.

SEPTEMBER 2, 1861

General Leonidas Polk--a native of neighboring Maury County, a bishop in the Episcopalian Church, and a kinsman to the former president--is given command over the Tennessee, Arkansas, and Missouri theaters in the early days of the War Between the States.

Leonidas Polk, an Episcopalian minister, was also a Confederate general.

SEPTEMBER 3, 1900

Executives of the Louisville and Nashville Railroad gather with those of the Nashville, Chattanooga and St. Louis Railroad to watch Engine Number 5 pull out of Union Station, Nashville's headquarters and depot for the two rail lines. The complex was begun twenty-five months earlier, and the final cost is one-half million dollars.

SEPTEMBER 4, 1813

Andrew Jackson and Thomas Hart Benton shoot it out in a gunfight on Nashville's Public Square. The squabble sends Benton packing to Missouri where he eventually indelibly links his name with America's westward expansion. Jackson, gravely wounded by one of the gunshots, stays in Nashville and becomes the town's leading citizen.

"Uncle" Alfred Jackson, personal body servant to Andrew Jackson.

SEPTEMBER 5, 1901

"Uncle" Alfred Jackson, Andrew Jackson's personal body-servant for many years, lies in state in the front hall of the Hermitage. According to his wishes, the former slave is buried in the gardens next to his beloved master.

SEPTEMBER 6. 1794

With the settlers' lives in the Cumberland Valley practically unbearable because of frequent Indians attacks, General James Robertson, disobeying the mandate of President George Washington, orders an armed expedition to march to the lower Cherokee towns on the Tennessee River and destroy them.

SEPTEMBER 7, 1891

Twenty thousand members of organized labor parade through Nashville streets to celebrate the American working man. Led

by Governor John Price Buchanan, the demonstration antici-
pates the Nation's official "Labor Day," set aside by Congress,
by three years.

SEPTEMBER 8, 1960

Wilma Rudolph wins her third gold medal at the Rome
Olympics.

SEPTEMBER 9, 1892

Nashville-born astronomer, Edward E. Barnard, discovers the
fifth moon of the planet, Jupiter, while working at the Lick
Observatory in California. Barnard, born on Patterson Street
near today's Baptist Hospital, goes on to become senior
astronomer at world-famous Yerkes Observatory, located in
Williams Bay, Wisconsin.

SEPTEMBER 10, 1894

Women from all over the South gather in Nashville and
establish the first chapter of the newly-organized United
Daughters of the Confederacy. Within months additional
chapters are formed in Savannah, Georgia; Wilmington,
North Carolina; Charleston, South Carolina; Jackson,
Tennessee; and Dallas, Texas. The women pledge to "culti-
vate ties of friendship among our women whose fathers,
brothers, sons, and mothers shared common dangers, suffer-
ings, and privations; and to instruct and instill into the
descendants of the people of the South a proper respect for
and pride in the glorious War history."

SEPTEMBER 11, 1806

Residents of Nashville, probably numbering no more than
1,500, incorporate their town. Joseph Coleman is elected as

the first mayor. The principal places of business still cluster around the Public Square, which also sports the jail, court house, and a couple of hotels.

SEPTEMBER 12, 1860

Nashville's infamous soldier of fortune, William Walker, is executed by a Honduran firing squad.

The destruction of Nickajack.

SEPTEMBER 13, 1794

General James Robertson and his Nashvillians attack the Indian towns of Nickajack and Running Water, both located on the middle stretch of the Tennessee River. Peace in the Cumberland River valley is finally assured.

SEPTEMBER 14, 1901

Theodore Roosevelt, a visitor to Nashville and the surrounding region while he researched his book, *Winning of the West*, becomes President of the United States, following William McKinley's assassination.

SEPTEMBER 15, 1862

War-time inflation hits Nashville. Coffee sells for eighty cents a pound, sugar is forty cents a pound, and butter brings one dollar a pound. Residential fences are torn down for firewood, which fetches twelve dollars a cord. By December, wood will bring up to thirty dollars a cord.

SEPTEMBER 16, 1838

The Reverend Richard Miles is consecrated to the post of Bishop of the Diocese of Nashville. Shortly afterwards, Bishop Miles reveals his plans for the city's first cathedral, Saint Mary's, to be built at the corner of present-day Fifth Avenue and Charlotte Street. The structure will be designed by William Strickland, the architect for the State Capitol, and, upon its completion in 1847, will cost $47,000.

SEPTEMBER 17, 1904

Dan McGugin arrives in Nashville to assume football coaching duties at Vanderbilt University.

SEPTEMBER 18, 1947

Ernest Tubb, Minnie Pearl, and George Hay, among others, take the Grand Ole Opry to a packed house at Carnegie Hall in

Nashville's Carnegie Library.

New York City. No performance there since Frank Sinatra's has been such an overwhelming success.

SEPTEMBER 19, 1904

Nashville's Carnegie Library--one of more than 2,500 libraries scattered all over America and made possible by the philanthropy of the immigrant Scots steel magnate, Andrew Carnegie--opens its doors at the corner of Eighth Avenue and Union Street, a site that the Ben West Public Library occupies today.

SEPTEMBER 20, 1911

The Tennessee Suffragists' organization is formed at the Tulane Hotel in Nashville. The group will be a local unit that pushes the passage of the Women's Suffrage Amendment to the United States Constitution allowing women to vote.

Mrs. Guilford Dudley, Sr., the organizer of the local chapter of the Tennessee Suffrage League and a moving force in the State's ratification of the amendment to the Constitution allowing women to vote.

SEPTEMBER 21, 1925

The War Memorial Building in downtown Nashville is dedicated. The magnificent marble and granite building has taken two years and two million dollars to complete. Among the dignitaries taking part in the festivities are World War heroes, Colonel Luke Lea and Sergeant Alvin York.

SEPTEMBER 22, 1869

The world-famous Maxwell House Hotel, located on the corner of today's Fourth Avenue and Church Street, has its formal opening. Begun ten years earlier and delayed by the War Between the States, the building has alternatively served as a Confederate barracks, a Union hospital, and a Union prison.

SEPTEMBER 23, 1863

The United States Army's 12th Corps passes through Nashville on its way to relieve General William S. Rosecrans at Chattanooga.

The Maxwell House Hotel.

SEPTEMBER 24, 1902

Nashville's baseball team wins the Southern League pennant for the second year in a row.

SEPTEMBER 25, 1893

Dr. James H. Kirkland is installed as Chancellor of Vanderbilt University.

SEPTEMBER 26, 1780

A large force of colonial militia, including many from the region that sixteen years later will become the State of Tennessee, depart from Sycamore Shoals in present-day Carter County to face down an American loyalist army at Kings

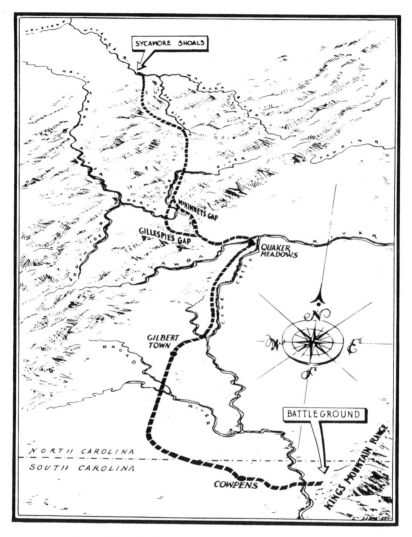

The trail from the Watauga Settlements to Kings Mountain.

Mountain in South Carolina. The militia's decisive victory over the loyalists produces the turning point of the Revolutionary War in the South.

SEPTEMBER 27, 1864

Nathan Bedford Forrest skirmishes Union forces in the Pulaski area, sixty miles south of Nashville.

SEPTEMBER 28, 1918

Influenza hits workers at the giant Du Pont powder plant at Old Hickory. Temporary hospitals are set up, as more than one hundred doctors and nurses arrive from nearby Nashville. The basement of the local YMCA, being used as a morgue, fills up with bodies faster than carts can carry them away. More than 1,300 Nashvillians die in the epidemic.

SEPTEMBER 29, 1863

The stairs at the partially completed Maxwell House Hotel-- now being used as a Union prison--collapse, killing twenty-one Confederate inmates.

SEPTEMBER 30, 1792

Fifteen riflemen battle between three and four hundred Cherokee and Creek Indians at Buchanan's Station, located on today's Elm Hill Pike near Donelson. During the heated conflict, Chiachattalla, the Creek leader, is killed, and John Watts, the Cherokee chief, is severely wounded in the hip. No defenders are injured.

The Battle at Buchanan's Station.

OCTOBER 1, 1827

Sam Houston, one of Nashville's most handsome and eligible bachelors, is inaugurated as Tennessee's seventh governor at the First Baptist Church. In the fall election, Houston had decisively defeated former Congressman Newton Cannon, a resident of Williamson County, by more than ten thousand votes. One of the new governor's proposals in his inaugural address is a canal on the Tennessee River "whereby the obstructions of the Muscle Shoals would be surmounted."

OCTOBER 2, 1927

Tennessee governor Austin Peay dies at the Governor's Residence on West End Avenue.

OCTOBER 3, 1883

The Vendome Theater, which in its years of glory will see offerings by many of the world's greatest performances, opens for business in a magnificent building on present-day Church Street between Sixth and Seventh Avenues. The opera, *Il Trovatore*, nets the theater five thousand dollars on opening day.

OCTOBER 4, 1899

The Medical Department of the University of Tennessee acquires a new building on Broad Street. Nashville now covers more than ten square miles and maintains 140 miles of improved streets. The city's population stands at nearly 81,000 people.

OCTOBER 5, 1896

The Democratic Party's candidate for president of the United States, William Jennings Bryan, speaks to an overflow crowd at the Ryman Auditorium. Bryan's message to Nashvillians is that a vote for the Democratic Party is a vote for "free coinage of silver" and "tariff for revenue only."

PULL FOR YOUR CANDIDATE

A campaign gimmick for William Jennings Bryan, sometimes called the "Silver Tongued Orator."

OCTOBER 6, 1783

Davidson becomes the first county to be established by the State of North Carolina in the middle section of the region that thirteen years later becomes Tennessee. The new entity is named in honor of North Carolina's General William Davidson, who was killed during the Revolution two years earlier.

OCTOBER 7, 1843

Following Knoxville, Murfreesboro, and Kingston, Nashville is made the capital of Tennessee. Actually, the legislature has met in Nashville since 1827, but permanent status is not granted until 1843. In order to snag the prize, Nashville officials

The Tennessee State Capitol during the 1880s.

purchase Campbell's Hill for $30,000 and present the property to the state for the construction of the capitol.

OCTOBER 8, 1878

Gideon Pillow, a University of Nashville graduate, former law partner of James K. Polk and a veteran of the Mexican War and the War Between the States, dies in Helena, Arkansas.

General Gideon Pillow fought in both the Mexican War and the War Between the States.

Nashville's magnificent Union Station at the turn of the century.

OCTOBER 9, 1900

Although it has already been in use for a month, Union Station now has its formal opening.

OCTOBER 10, 1843

The richest horse race yet to be held in the World, the $35,000 Peyton Stakes, is held at the Nashville Race Course, today's Metro Center. The winning horse is renamed "Peytona," in honor of the race's promoter, Bailie Peyton.

OCTOBER 11, 1811

A law is passed that increases the number of Nashville aldermen-- today's councilmen--from six to seven, with the proviso that when the town becomes large enough to split it into six wards, a total of twelve aldermen will be elected.

OCTOBER 12, 1835

Williamson Countian Newton Cannon, a former U. S. Congressman, is inaugurated as Tennessee's first Whig governor.

Governor Newton Cannon.

OCTOBER 13, 1823

An exasperated Nashville resident asks city aldermen, "why we have no fire companies, why some streets are improved to the exclusion of others, why some most abandoned characters are suffered to go at large and insult the better portion of our citizens with their gross immoralities, why gambling-houses and tippling shops, and all other nuisances are permitted to exist without restraint [and] why some of our public springs are allowed to become unfit for use for want of attention of them?"

OCTOBER 14, 1890

Gates P. Thruston, a former Union general who now makes his home in Nashville, receives the appreciation of the Tennessee Historical Society for his authorship of the best-selling book, *The Antiquities of Tennessee.*

OCTOBER 15, 1887

President and Mrs. Grover Cleveland arrive in Nashville aboard a special train from Memphis. General and Mrs. W. H.

Jackson of Belle Meade are the Clevelands' hosts. Before they leave Nashville the president and his lady visit Mrs. James K. Polk at Polk Place.

OCTOBER 16, 1905

The Vanderbilt football team defeats the University of Michigan by a score of 18 to 0.

OCTOBER 17, 1828

In reporting on what history calls the "Trail of Tears," the *Nashville Whig* recounts that the "second detachment of the emigrating Cherokees passed through Nashville...on their way to the 'Far West.' They lay encamped near Foster's mill on the Murfreesboro Turnpike for several days, and while there were visited by many of our citizens."

OCTOBER 18, 1890

Local newspapers urge that the State Prison be removed from Nashville.

OCTOBER 19, 1892

"Nancy Hanks," the renowned harness horse, maintains her world record in the Nashville races.

OCTOBER 20, 1865

Confederate guerrilla fighter, Champ Ferguson, sits in his cell at the State Prison on Church Street with only hours to live. Recently captured by Union troops, it comes as no surprise

The state prison on Church Street, where Champ Ferguson was hanged.

that Ferguson will hang. His final words are, "I killed a good many men, of course; I don't deny that, but never killed a man whom I did not know was seeking my life....I don't know some of the things in these specifications, but I don't deny anything I ever done...."

OCTOBER 21, 1891

Twelve thousand viewers watch "the greatest race on the American turf" at Cumberland Park, the site of the present-day State Fairgrounds. Edward F. Geers, a world-famous local horseman drives "Hal Pointer," from Maury County, and George Starr drives the California challenger, "Direct." "Direct" beats "Hal Pointer" in three heats with times of 2:10, 2:09 1/4, and 2:11, setting two world's records.

OCTOBER 22, 1907

More than 150,000 people greet President Theodore Roosevelt as he steps from his train at Union Station. Whistles blow all over the city and a twenty-one gun salute is fired from Capitol

President Theodore Roosevelt at the Hermitage.

Hill. TR speaks at the Ryman Auditorium and at Peabody College, before visiting the Hermitage. When he returns to Washington, Roosevelt personally steers a bill through Congress that appropriates federal funds to assist the Ladies' Hermitage Association in maintaining "Old Hickory's" home.

OCTOBER 23, 1863

Maury Countian, General Leonidas Polk, is relieved of his command of a corps in the Army of Tennessee.

OCTOBER 24, 1929

Prices on the New York Stock Exchange begin to fall rapidly. Five days later, panic sets in, much selling of stock is done, and large numbers of heavy investors find themselves penniless. Among the Nashvillians affected by the market's failure is Rogers Caldwell, who before the crash was reported to be worth more than six hundred million dollars, with an annual income of two and a half million.

OCTOBER 25, 1909

The Henshaw Grand Opera Company opens at the Ryman Auditorium with selections from *Faust*, *Carmen*, and *Romeo and Juliet*.

OCTOBER 26, 1799

Williamson County is established. Its lands are derived from the southern part of Davidson County. Franklin is named the seat of government for the new county which is named in honor of Dr. Hugh Williamson of North Carolina. At the same legislative session, Wilson and Smith Counties are also organized.

OCTOBER 27, 1859

An article in the *Louisville Journal* describes a trip to Nashville on the Louisville and Nashville Railroad. "It was after five o'clock before we reached Nashville, and in the golden flood of the sunset, it presented a beautiful appearance--the new Capitol, the most conspicuous object in the distance, and the suspension bridge over the Cumberland River, poised in airy lightness like a telegraph wire...."

OCTOBER 28, 1843

Former Nashville and Franklin resident, John Sappington, a physician who earlier migrated to Missouri with his family, copyrights the first medical book ever published west of the Mississippi River. Sappington, already known for his miracle pills that cure malaria, entitles his book, *The Theory and Treatment of Fevers.*

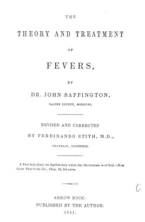

Title-page to Dr. John Sappington's book. Sappington was assisted in his efforts by Dr. Ferdinando Stith of Franklin.

OCTOBER 29, 1907

The Nashville Clearing House limits bank withdrawals to fifty dollars a week following the stock market tumble on Wall Street.

OCTOBER 30, 1945

The Children's Museum, precursor to today's Cumberland Museum, opens for business in a building located in South Nashville that once housed classrooms for the University of Nashville.

OCTOBER 31, 1847

The *Nashville Daily Union* reports on the consecration of St. Mary's Church. The news article reveals that "on Sunday, the 31st, a large body of our fellow-citizens witnessed a noble and imposing spectacle--the dedication of the new Catholic Cathedral just completed. This beautiful edifice situated on the corner of Cedar and Summer Streets, is an ornament to our city."

A William Strickland masterpiece, St. Mary's Cathedral.
Consecrated October 31, 1847

NOVEMBER 1, 1880

Grantland Rice, hailed by many as the greatest sportswriter of all time and a one-time Nashville newspaperman, is born in Murfreesboro. Rice will go on to be educated in Nashville at the Wallace School and at Vanderbilt University.

Internationally known sportswriter, Grantland Rice (second from left), and Vanderbilt's Dan McGugin (right).

Young man dressed to play football at the turn of the century.

NOVEMBER 2, 1907

Avenging their 1905 defeat at the hands of Vanderbilt, the University of Michigan football team beats the Commodores by a score of 8 to 0.

NOVEMBER 3, 1948

The country awakens thinking that Thomas Dewey has defeated President Harry Truman in the presidential election. One newspaper, the *Chicago Daily News*, actually prints an edition with screaming headlines that proclaim, "Dewey Defeats Truman." Actually, President Truman wins the contest with 303 electoral votes to Dewey's 189, and he carries Tennessee by a margin of 68,000 votes.

NOVEMBER 4, 1902

James B. Frazier, a Democrat, defeats both the Republican and Prohibitionist candidates in the Tennessee governor's race.

NOVEMBER 5, 1912

Shortly after midnight, the walls of the city reservoir, perched high upon Kirkpatrick Hill just off of Eighth Avenue, South, break, releasing twenty-five million gallons of water into the surrounding neighborhood. Miraculously, no one is seriously injured, but three feet of mud stand in Eighth Avenue.

The Nashville Resorvoir on Eighth Avenue, South, at the turn of the century.

NOVEMBER 6, 1860

Nashvillians turn out in record numbers to vote for locally-born John Bell for the presidency of the United States. Bell, a former congressman, speaker of the U. S. House of Representatives, United States secretary of war, and U. S. senator handily carries Tennessee over his three illustrious opponents-- Abraham Lincoln, Stephen A. Douglas, and John C. Breckinridge.

Presidential candidate John Bell of Nashville.

NOVEMBER 7, 1803

The U. S. Mail from New Orleans and Natchez arrives one day late in Nashville. Orders go out to the various post offices along the way demanding "that you will invariably dispatch the carrier from your office at the stipulated hour, without waiting for the arrival of the depending mail; and at all times be prepared to forward by express such mail as fails in arriving at your office, at the proper period, to meet the proper carrier.... The mail must in no instance be detained over five minutes at any post office...."

A mail carrier on the Natchez Trace.

NOVEMBER 8, 1864

President Abraham Lincoln is re-elected president of the United States, with Tennessean Andrew Johnson, as his vice-president.

NOVEMBER 9, 1908

Former U. S. senator and prominent newspaperman, Edward Ward Carmack, is gunned down on Seventh Avenue near Union Street. The murderers, Duncan B. Cooper and his son, Robin, testify that they killed Carmack because of his offensive newspaper editorials. The Coopers receive sentences of twenty years each in prison. Robin Cooper's appeal to the Supreme Court results in a new trial, while his father's conviction is upheld. However,

Edward Ward Carmack.

before further action can be taken, Governor Malcolm Patterson pardons both men, creating a furor across the state.

NOVEMBER 10, 1890

P. T. Barnum's pride and joy, Mrs. Tom Thumb, standing barely thirty-five inches tall, performs for delighted Nashville children at the Vendome Theater.

NOVEMBER 11, 1924

Famed evangelist, Billy Sunday, preaches at Nashville's Haymarket Square. Ironically, an older generation of

Nashvillians had witnessed Sunday, then a center fielder for Chicago, play in an exhibition game against the home baseball team, the Nashville Americans, at the new ball park, Sulphur Dell, in April, 1885.

NOVEMBER 12, 1908

Edward Ward Carmack, shot down in cold blood in Nashville three days earlier, is laid to rest in Columbia, Tennessee.

NOVEMBER 13, 1833

During the early morning hours, hundreds of Nashvillians observe a magnificent meteor shower. The event is recorded by history as "the night the stars fell." One eyewitness exclaims that he "arose and looked from the window into the southern heavens at 30 minutes past 4 a.m. and witnessed a sight unlike any thing I had seen before, and impressive in the extreme....it more resembled a shower of small balls of white flame than any other appearance with which it can be compared...."

NOVEMBER 14, 1814

Six women and one man organize one of the city's first Presbyterian churches on the Public Square.

NOVEMBER 15, 1896

Captain Tom Ryman launches a new steamboat, the *H. W. Buttorff*, on the Cumberland River at Nashville.

NOVEMBER 16, 1862

Prominent Nashville architect, Adolphus Heiman, dies as a result of impaired health brought about by Union imprisonment after the fall of Fort Donelson. A native of Prussia, Heiman's architectural designs included the University of Nashville, the old Davidson County jail, and the Insane Asylum on Murfreesboro Road.

Adolphus Heiman, after whom Heiman Street in North Nashville is named.

NOVEMBER 17, 1893

William Smith, a Nashville architect, presents his ideas for a Centennial Exposition to celebrate Tennessee's one hundredth birthday to interested members of the Commercial Club.

NOVEMBER 18, 1786

Neighboring Sumner County is established by the North Carolina Assembly. Its lands come from Davidson County, and its name is in honor of General Jethro Sumner, a Revolutionary War general.

NOVEMBER 19, 1843

Nashville's William Walker, who will one day be elected to the presidency of Nicaragua, continues his education in Paris, France. The following day, he writes to his friend in Nashville,

John Berrien Lindsley, that "More than six months have elapsed since I landed in Europe; and my visit has already had a great influence on many of my opinions. It has made me more of an American than ever--more fond of my country's institutions, and prouder of her history and her resources."

NOVEMBER 20, 1863

Sam Davis, a young Confederate soldier from nearby Smyrna who attended school at the Montgomery Bell Academy in Nashville, is captured by enemy forces near Pulaski. Davis is tried by Union authorities as a spy and, when he refuses to divulge information about his organization, he is sentenced to be executed one week later. His final

Sam Davis, boy hero.

words are "If I had a thousand lives, I would rather lose them all before I would betray my friends or the confidence of my informer."

NOVEMBER 21, 1788

Mr. E. Bushnell, a native of Connecticut who has recently visited Middle Tennessee, writes in a letter to his local newspaper that "The Cumberland is a gentle stream about the size of the Connecticut river. The soil exceeds my highest expectations. Oats and barley flourish exceedingly. Flax, hemp, cotton and tobacco grow luxuriantly, and no part of Vermont can exceed this country for grass; vegetables of every kind grow here in great abundance. The temperature of the climate is such, that stock support themselves in the woods, during the winter months, and keep in fine order."

NOVEMBER 22, 1897

The City of Nashville presents a magnificent silver service to the officers of the gunboat, *U. S. S. Nashville.*

NOVEMBER 23, 1892

Fifty thousand spectators watch as a torchlight parade celebrating the Democratic party victories in the November 8 elections winds through the downtown streets of Nashville.

NOVEMBER 24, 1904

Vanderbilt beats the Sewanee team in football, 26 to 0. The crowd, more than 5,000, sets a state record for attendance at a college football game.

NOVEMBER 25, 1895

An inclined bicycle track, reported to be one of the finest in the country, opens at Nashville's Coliseum.

NOVEMBER 26, 1904

Lock and Dam A on the Cumberland River below Nashville is dedicated. The lock and dam will allow river traffic to pass the treacherous water at Harpeth Shoals with little difficulty.

Sulphur Dell Baseball Park, located just north of the State Capitol.

NOVEMBER 27, 1890

Hundreds of Nashvillians watch the city's first football game at Sulphur Dell baseball park. Vanderbilt beats Peabody by a score of 40 to 0.

NOVEMBER 28, 1785

The Treaty of Hopewell is signed in South Carolina between representatives of the Cherokee Indians and the United States government. The treaty makes official the transfer of the land upon which Nashville is located from the Cherokees to the United States.

NOVEMBER 29, 1899

The First Tennessee Regiment, back from brief service in the Spanish-American War, arrives in Nashville.

The Carter gin house, scene of some of the bloodiest fighting at Franklin.

NOVEMBER 30, 1864

The Battle of Franklin, a prelude to General John Bell Hood's attempt to win back Nashville for the Confederacy, is fought. Often termed the bloodiest battle of the War Between the States, the conflict at Franklin rages for nearly five hours and results in thousands of casualties on both sides. Five Confederate generals are killed, six others wounded--one mortally--and one other is taken prisoner. The outcome is indecisive.

DECEMBER 1, 1890

The Vine Street Christian Church on Seventh Avenue, North, is dedicated.

The Vine Street Christian Church.

DECEMBER 2, 1864

After the disastrous battle at Franklin on November 30, advance units of General John Bell Hood's Army of Tennessee check out the Union defenses at Nashville.

DECEMBER 3, 1872

After being used as a Union hospital during the War Between the States, the St. Cloud Hotel, located at present-day Fifth Avenue and Church Street, reopens for business.

DECEMBER 4, 1895

Lillian Russell performs at the Vendome Theater in Nashville.

DECEMBER 5, 1907

Nashville's mayor urges officials to fund the electrification of the city's street railroads in order to eliminate pollution.

DECEMBER 6, 1900

The Vienna Orchestra entertains hundreds of Nashvillians during a concert at the Union Gospel Tabernacle on Fifth Avenue, North.

DECEMBER 7, 1941

Nashville aviatrix, Cornelia Fort, while teaching a student pilot high above Hawaii, is one of the first Americans to spot incoming Japanese airplanes. When Miss Fort is accidentally killed in 1943, she becomes the first woman pilot to die in the service of her country.

DECEMBER 8, 1937

The present-day Davidson County Court House on Nashville's Public Square is dedicated. Built at a cost of one and a half million dollars, the structure is the design of the Nashville architectural firm of Emmons Woolwine.

John Berrien Lindsley.

DECEMBER 9, 1897

John Berrien Lindsley, sometimes called "the Benjamin Franklin of

Nashville," dies. Lindsley, an eminent physician, educator, and author, was instrumental in the founding of the University of Nashville Medical School and George Peabody College for Teachers.

DECEMBER 10, 1864

Inclement weather at Nashville prevents Union General George Thomas from attacking General John Bell Hood's Confederate army poised on the outskirts of town.

DECEMBER 11, 1942

Hundreds of happy, black Baptists watch as the mortgage papers to the Morris Building, located on the corner of Fourth Avenue and Charlotte Street, are burned. The structure, begun in 1924 and dedicated five years later, is at last the property of the National Baptist Convention, USA, the largest black owned and operated religious publishing house in the world.

DECEMBER 12, 1891

Mark Twain's *The Prince and the Pauper*, is performed at the Vendome Theater.

DECEMBER 13, 1919

Former Nashville painter, Gilbert Gaul, described as "the most capable of American military painters," dies in New York. Gaul, noted for his sensitive portrayals of scenes during the War Between the States, was internationally known when he moved to Nashville in 1905.

One of Gilbert Gaul's most popular works,
Leaving Home.

DECEMBER 14, 1864

General George Thomas, the Union commander at Nashville, advises his superiors in Washington that he will attack General John Bell Hood's Confederate army the following day.

DECEMBER 15, 1864

The last great battle of the War Between the States begins. The "decisive" engagement at Nashville will be the Army of Tennessee's last major effort to regain lost ground and to end the agonizing three and a half year-long conflict. Outnumbered, outgunned, and out-supplied, Hood's ragtag army tries for two days, in frigid cold and snow, to out-maneuver the superior forces of Thomas. On the following day, Hood retreats south.

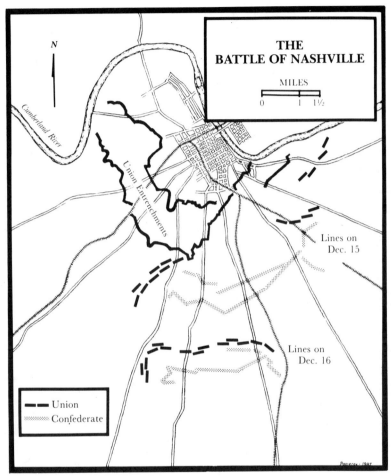

Plan of the Battle of Nashville.

DECEMBER 16, 1811

The New Madrid earthquake, judged by most scientists to be the worst set of tremors ever to hit North America, sends shock waves through Nashville. A building under construction on the Public Square shakes so much that workmen refuse to return to their jobs. An eleven-year old eyewitness recalls years later that his father called all the children down from upstairs for fear the house would tumble.

DECEMBER 17, 1905

The Southern Turf Saloon, a fine gentlemen's club and saloon located on Fourth Avenue between Union and Church Streets, advertises its whiskey for four, five, and six dollars a gallon.

DECEMBER 18, 1801

The Treaty of Fort Adams, signed by authorities with represent atives of the Choctaw Indians, allows the federal government to begin work on the Natchez Trace Road. The thoroughfare will follow the old Natchez Trace from Natchez, Mississippi Territory to Nashville. The Choctaws are paid two thousand dollars worth of merchandise and three sets of blacksmithing tools for the road's right-of-way.

DECEMBER 19, 1840

Famed Nashville attorney and statesman, Felix Grundy, dies. While a member of the U. S. House of Representatives, he became one of America's leading proponents for America's entry into the War of 1812 with Great Britain. Grundy later served in the U. S. Senate and as President Martin Van Buren's attorney general. In

Felix Grundy, who, in his time, was one of the most influential men in the United States.

Nashville, he built and lived in a palatial home near today's Seventh Avenue and Union Street that was later purchased and used by former President and Mrs. James K. Polk.

DECEMBER 20, 1864

General John Bell Hood's retreating Confederate army skirmishes with Union troops near Columbia. Hood's soldiers destroy the town's bridges.

DECEMBER 21, 1864

Union troops pursue Hood's Army of Tennessee near Pulaski.

DECEMBER 22, 1828

Rachel Jackson, the beloved wife of President-elect Andrew Jackson, dies at the Hermitage. Rachel, a daughter of John Donelson, one of Nashville's co-founders, had arrived at Fort Nashborough in April, 1780 aboard her father's flatboat, the *Adventure*. Rachel's life with Jackson, particularly during the past few months of campaigning by her husband, was marred by constant rumors by

Rachel Donelson Jackson

Jackson's political enemies that her first marriage was not dissolved legally. The grieved Jackson has carved on her monument that "a being so gentle and yet so virtuous slander might wound, but could not dishonor."

DECEMBER 23, 1904

Legislation renaming downtown Nashville's north-south streets is considered by Mayor Albert Williams. The following day, the mayor signs the bill into law. Thus, the original colorful names of the city's streets--Water, Market, College, Cherry, Summer, High, Vine, and Spruce, all named after Philadelphia streets except College and High--are changed to the common-place First through Eighth Avenue, respectively.

One of the buildings comprising the University of Nashville on present-day Second Avenue, South.

DECEMBER 24, 1824

Phillip Lindsley, father of John Berrien Lindsley, is installed as president of Cumberland College, later to be known as the University of Nashville. Lindsley comes to Nashville from the temporary presidency of Princeton University. During his twenty-three year tenure in Nashville, his college's list of graduates will read like a "who's who" of Nashville.

The James Robertson party arriving at the site of Nashville.

DECEMBER 25, 1779

James Robertson's overland party of men, boys, and livestock arrives at the Bluffs, site of future Nashville, after crossing the Cumberland River on the ice.

DECEMBER 26, 1904

The Union Gospel Tabernacle is renamed the Ryman Auditorium in honor of Captain Tom Ryman who died three days earlier. Ryman, a steamboat captain, had donated twenty thousand dollars toward the construction of the building in 1881. Sam Jones, the noted revivalist who had converted Ryman almost a quarter of a century earlier, returns to Nashville to conduct the funeral. A local newspaper calls Ryman "an honest man and earnest Christian."

The Ryman Auditorium shortly after it was renamed.

DECEMBER 27, 1850

The locomotive, *Tennessee*, makes its maiden run in South Nashville. The *Nashville True Whig* reports that "The new locomotive, 'Tennessee' was put 'in gear'...and made a trial trip of a mile out the Nashville and Chattanooga Railroad. The little excursion was witnessed with much interest by a number of speculators, some of whom 'took passage.' It marks an era in our history."

DECEMBER 28, 1863

Union troops operate against Confederate guerrilla activity in the area.

DECEMBER 29, 1808

Andrew Johnson, one of Tennessee's future governors--and its only military governor, as well as president of the United States--is born in North Carolina.

DECEMBER 30, 1926

Record flood waters from the overflowing Cumberland River engulf Nashville. Merchants on lower Broad Street and on First, Second, and Third Avenues are inundated. Flood waters climb to 56.2 feet, 16.2 feet over flood stage. The river in some places stretches to three miles in width.

First Avenue, South and Broad Street during the 1926-1927 floods.

DECEMBER 31, 1862

The Battle of Stone's River (Murfreesboro) begins. The bloody conflict will last for three days, and when it is over, Confederate General Braxton Bragg will fall back south along the Duck River, leaving much of rural Middle Tennessee again in the hands of Union forces.

THE END

CREDITS & CAPTIONS
FOR ILLUSTRATIONS USED IN

On This Day . . .

A Year in the Life of Nashville and Middle Tennessee

January 4, 1919 -*Colonel Luke Lea and the team assembled to kidnap Kaiser Wilhelm during the opening days of 1919. Seated left to right: Captain Leland S. McPhail of Nashville, later the controversial owner of the Brooklyn Dodgers and the New York Yankees; Colonel Luke Lea; Captain Thomas P. Henderson of Franklin; and Lieutenant Ellsworth Brown, hometown unknown. Standing left to right: Sergeant Dan Reilly of Williamson County; Sergeant Toliver, hometown unknown; Sergeant Owen Johnston of Williamson County; and Corporal Marmaduke Clokey, hometown unknown.*
Photo courtesy of **Tom Henderson**.

January 6, 1818 - *General Andrew Jackson as he appeared during the War of 1812. Portrait from* **The Pageant of America**.

January 8, 1815 - *Andrew Jackson and his men at the Battle of New Orleans. Drawing from* **McGee's A History of Tennessee**.

January 9, 1866 - *Jubilee Hall at Fisk University as it appeared in 1907. Photo from* **Nashville, the Gateway of the South**.

January 11, 1781 - *Felix Robertson, first white child born in Nashville. Portrait courtesy of the* **Tennessee Historical Society**.

January 15, 1786 - *An artist's conception of John Donelson. No likeness is known to exist. Drawing by* **Jim Farrell**.

January 17, 1979 - *Governor Lamar Alexander.*

January 18, 1792 - *Sevier's Blockhouse. Skeetch from* **James A. Crutchfield**.

January 22, 1829 - *Sam Houston as an older man after he had left Tennessee and made his mark in Texas. Drawing from* **McGee's A History of Tennessee**.

January 27, 1830 - *Senator Thomas Hart Benton of Missouri, formerly a resident of Williamson County and one-time protege of Andrew Jackson. Portrait from* **Benton's Thirty Years' View**.

January 28, 1845 - *President James K. Polk. Portrait courtesy of the U. S.* **Bureau of Engraving**.

January 29, 1902 - *The original St. Thomas Hospital on Hayes Street, as it appeared in 1907. Photo from* **Nashville, The Gateway of the South**.

February 7, 1849 - *Zachary Taylor, popular Mexican War hero and president-elect of the United States. Portrait courtesy of the* **U. S. Bureau of Engraving.**

February 11, 1862 - *Confederate General Simon Bolivar Buckner. Photo from* **Miller's The Photographic History of the Civil War.**

February 15, 1791 - *William Blount, governor of the Territory of the United States, South of the River Ohio, commonly called the Southwest Territory, the precursor to Tennessee. Drawing from* **McGee's A History of Tennessee**

February 16, 1862 - *Fort Donelson under attack by Union gunboats. Engraving from* **Harper's Pictorial History of the Civil War.**

February 18, 1862 - *The wooden covered bridge over the Cumberland River at Nashville that was burned by the city's residents. Engraving from* **Harper's Pictorial History of the Civil War.**

February 20, 1918 - *Theater poster for Mrs. Ziegfeld's new edition of the Follies. Photo courtesy of the* **Nashville Public Library.**

February 21, 1854 - *One of Mark Cockrill's prize Merino sheep. Drawing from* **The Pageant of America.**

February 25, 1862 - *Nashville residents read Mayor R. B. Cheatham's proclamation surrendering Nashville to Union forces under General Don Carlos Buell. Drawing from* **Harper's Pictorial History of the Civil War.**

February 26, 1856 - *The original Hume School. Photo courtesy of the* **Tennessee State Library and Archives.**

February 29, 1900
Map of Nashville around the turn of the twentieth century. From the **author's collection.**

March 6, 1885
Samuel Watkins. Drawing by **Jim Farrell.**

March 13, 1905 - *Entrance to Mt. Olivet Cemetery, final resting place of General William Bate. Photo from* **Art Work of Nashville**

March 17, 1775 - *Richard Henderson's land notice advertising for potential settlers in present-day Middle Tennessee. Picture from* **The Pageant of America**

March 19, 1859 - *The Tennessee State Capitol Building, designed by Philadelphia architect, William Strickland. Photo from* **Nashville, the Gateway of the South.**

March 22, 1916 - *Charred remains of buildings destroyed in the East Nashville fire of March 22, 1916. Photo courtesy of the* **Tennessee State Library and Archives.**

March 24, 1864 - *General Nathan Bedford Forrest, the "Wizard of the Saddle," ranks among the most brilliant cavalry commanders the world has ever seen. Drawing from* **McGee's A History of Tennessee.**

March 26, 1873 - *Vanderbilt University, pictured several years after its founding, sits atop Litton Hill off West End Avenue. Drawing courtesy of* **Carl Zibart.**

March 27, 1814 - *Sam Houston, having a barbed arrow removed forcefully from his thigh, at the battle of Horseshoe Bend. Drawing from* **Garrett's and Goodpasture's History of Tennessee.**

March 29, 1867 - *The Ku Klux Klan was founded in Pulaski, Tennessee in late 1866. Drawing from* **McGee's A History of Tennessee.**

March 31, 1851 - *The "Swedish Nightingale," Jenny Lind. Portrait from* **The Pageant of America.**

April 2, 1781 - *The Battle of the Bluffs, in which Charlotte Robertson saved the day by releasing Fort Nashborough's dogs upon the Indians. Engraving from* **McGee's A History of Tennessee.**

April 3, 1877 - *The giant balloon, Carnival, draws curious onlookers to Nashville's Public Square. Photo courtesy of the* **Tennessee State Library and Archives.**

April 5, 1865 - *William Gannaway "Parson" Brownlow. Drawing from* **McGee's A History of Tennessee.**

April 6, 1919 - *Thousands of Nashvillians cheer returning heroes from the Great War in Europe. Photo courtesy of the* **Tennessee State Library and Archives.**

April 7, 1831 - *Franklin resident John H. Eaton. Portrait from* **Heiskell's Andrew Jackson**

April 9, 1766 - *John Overton's home, Traveller's Rest, shown during the War Between the States when it was used as a command post by General John Bell Hood. Drawing from* **Century Magazine.**

April 10, 1886 - *Testing the strength of the Woodland Street Bridge.*
Photo courtesy of the **Nashville Chamber of Commerce***.*

April 16, 1829 - *Hall's Station in Sumner County, where Governor William Hall*
was raised amidst continuous Indian troubles.
Photo from **Early History of the South-West**

April 18, 1810 - *Alexander Wilson, the eminent painter.*
Portrait from the painting by **Rembrandt Peale***.*

April 24, 1780 - *The arrival at Fort Nashborough of John Donelson's riverparty.*
Painting by **Sandor Bodo***, courtesy of* **First Tennessee Bank***.*

May 3, 1897 - *Opening day at the Tennessee Centennial Celebration.*
Photo courtesy of **Carl Zibart***.*

May 4, 1825 - *General Lafayette, who had greatly assisted in the American war*
effort against Great Britain during the Revolution.
Engraving from **Dover's The American Revolution: A Picture Sourcebook***.*

May 7, 1890 - *Sergeant George Jordan, Williamson County's contribution to the*
famed "Buffalo Soldiers." Drawing by **Frederic Remington***.*

May 13, 1797 - *Louis Philippe visited Nashville several years before he was*
crowned King of France. Portrait courtesy of the **Comte de Paris***.*

May 16, 1771 - *The Battle of Alamance, referred to by some historians as the first*
battle of the American Revolution. Engraving from **McGee's A History of**
Tennessee*.*

May 18, 1938 - *The official emblem of the Natchez Trace Parkway.*
Courtesy of the **National Park Service***.*

May 20, 1880 - *Thousands watch at the unveiling of Andrew Jackson's statue on the*
State Capitol grounds. Photo courtesy of the **Tennessee State Library and**
Archives*.*

May 27, 1865 - *President Andrew Johnson.*
Engraving courtesy of the U. S. **Bureau of Engraving***.*

May 28, 1907 - *Jere Baxter, founder of the Tennessee Central Railroad.*
Portrait from **Wooldridge's History of Nashville***.*

May 29, 1805 - *Former Vice-president Aaron Burr.*
*Portrait from **The Pageant of America**.*

June 1, 1796 - *John Sevier, first governor of the State of Tennessee.*
*Drawing from **McGee's A History of Tennessee**.*

June 8, 1861 - *Isham G. Harris, Tennessee's war-time governor.*
*Drawing from **McGee's A History of Tennessee**.*

June 9, 1819 - *Nashville Female Academy, located on the site of downtown*
Nashville's YMCA at Ninth Avenue and Church Street.
*Photo courtesy of the **Tennessee State Museum**.*

June 11, 1843 - *Nashville's beloved Charlotte Reeves Robertson, wife of the town's*
*founder. Drawing by **Jim Farrell**.*

June 13, 1922 - *Murfreesboro and Nashville writer Mary Noailles Murfree.*
*Drawing by **Jim Farrell**.*

June 15, 1849 - *Polk Place in Nashville, the last home of President James K. Polk.*
*Photo courtesy of the **Tennessee State Library and Archives**.*

June 17, 1861 - *The Confederate "Stars and Bars."*
*Drawing from **McGee's A History of Tennessee**.*

June 19, 1845 - *William Strickland, designer of the Tennessee State Capitol.*
*Portrait courtesy of the **Tennessee State Museum**.*

June 21, 1904 - *The J. B. Richardson (left), one of Captain Tom Ryman's steam-*
*boats, docked at the foot of Broad Street. Photo courtesy of **Marine Photo***
***Company**.*

June 24, 1936 - *Berry Field, Nashville's commercial airport for many years prior*
to the opening of the new Nashville International.
*Photo courtesy of the **Nashville Chamber of Commerce**.*

July 2, 1839 - *Belmont, the home of Adelicia and Joseph Acklen, one of the South's*
*premier estates. Photo from **Art Work of Nashville**.*

July 4, 1892 - *Bicycling was a popular sport in Nashville near the turn of the centu-*
*ry. Painting by **Carl Rakeman**, Courtesy of the **Federal Highway Commission**.*

July 5, 1830 - *Christ Episcopal Church at the corner of Ninth Avenue and Broad*
*Street.Photo from **Nashville, the Gateway of the South**.*

July 9, 1918 - *Dutchman's Curve, located under present-day White Bridge Road, the site of the nation's worst railway accident.*
Photo courtesy of the **Nashville Public Library**.

July 12, 1856 - *William Walker--physician, lawyer, newspaperman, soldier of fortune.Drawing from* **McGee's A History of Tennessee**.

July 18, 1830 - *Margaret "Peggy" Eaton, wife of Franklin's John H. Eaton.*
Photo by **Matthew Brady**, *courtesy of the* **Library of Congress**.

July 25, 1903 - *The old Duncan Hotel which once stood on the corner of present-day Fourth Avenue and Charlotte Street.*
Photo from **Nashville, the Gateway of the South**.

July 29, 1924 - *One of Nashville's earlier airports, Blackwood Field.*
Photo courtesy of the **Tennessee State Library and Archives**.

July 30, 1887 - *Belle Meade, the "queen" of Southern plantations.*
Photo from **Art Work of Nashville**.

July 31, 1797 - *Title-page from Francis Baily's book documenting his American travels, including his trip up the Natchez Trace to Nashville.*
From the author's collection.

August 1, 1787 - *James Robertson, founder of Nashville.*
Drawing from **McGee's A History of Tennessee**.

August 12, 1862 - *John Hunt Morgan, the Confederate guerrilla fighter.*
Photo from **Miller's The Photographic History of the Civil War**.

August 14, 1891 - *Mrs. James Knox Polk, the first lady of Nashville for many years after her husband's death. Drawing from* **Frank Leslie's Illustrated Magazine**.

August 16, 1977 - *Elvis Presley was one of the first American musicians to be honored by a postage stamp. Courtesy of the U. S.* **Postal Service**

August 18, 1856 - *The U. S. Customs House, still standing, that was so long coming to Nashville. Photo from* **Nashville, the Gateway of the South**.

August 20, 1852 - *Felix Zollicoffer survived his duel only to be killed in action during the War Between the States.*
Portrait from **Miller's The Photographic History of the Civil War**.

August 22, 1800 - *General William Selby Harney was called "The Hornet" by his Teton Sioux foes because of his relentless pursuit of them during the Plains Indian wars of the 1850s. From an **old photograph.***

August 25, 1960 - *Wilma Rudolph and a photo of the 1956 A & I women's Olympic team, with Coach Ed Temple in the middle. Photo by **Joe Zinn.***

August 28, 1802 - *Title-page of F. A. Michaux's book about his travels to America, including his trip to Nashville and vicinity in 1802. From the **author's collection.***

August 31, 1875 - *Frank and Jesse James were already wanted men when Jesse's son was born in Edgefield (East Nashville). **An old reward poster.***

September 2, 1861 - *Leonidas Polk, an Episcopalian minister, was also a Confederate general. Drawing from **McGee's A History of Tennessee.***

September 4, 1813 - *The Jackson--Benton gunfight at the City Hotel on Nashville's Public Square. Drawing by **Charles Young.***

September 5, 1901 - *"Uncle" Alfred Jackson, personal body servant to Andrew Jackson. Photo courtesy of **Carl Zibart.***

September 9, 1892 - *Edward E. Barnard, recognized the world over for his accomplishments in astronomy and celestial photography. Drawing by **Jim Farrell.***

September 13, 1794 - *The destruction of Nickajack. Drawing from **Dover's The American Revolution: A Picture Sourcebook.***

September 19, 1904 - *Nashville's Carnegie Library. Photo from **Nashville, the Gateway of the South.***

September 20, 1911 - *Mrs. Guilford Dudley, Sr., the organizer of the local chapter of the Tennessee Suffrage League and a moving force in the State's ratification of the amendment to the Constitution allowing women to vote. Photo courtesy of **Carl Zibart.***

September 22, 1869 - *The Maxwell House Hotel. Photo from **Nashville, the Gateway of the South.***

September 26, 1780 - *The trail from the Watauga Settlements to Kings Mountain. Map from **National Park Service Historical Handbook Series No. 22.***

September 30, 1792 - *The Battle at Buchanan's Station. Engraving from **Kendall's Life of Andrew Jackson.***

October 5, 1896 --*A campaign gimmick for William Jennings Bryan, sometimes called the "Silver Tongued Orator." Courtesy* **Smithsonian Institution.**

October 7, 1843 - The Tennessee State Capitol during the 1880s. Engraving from **McGee's A History of Tennessee.**

October 8, 1878 - General Gideon Pillow fought in both the Mexican War and the War Between the States. Photo from **Miller's The Photographic History of the Civil War.**

October 9, 1900 - Nashville's magnificent Union Station at the turn of the century. Photo from **Nashville, the Gateway of the South.**

October 12, 1835 - Governor Newton Cannon. Drawing from **McGee's A History of Tennessee.**

October 14, 1890 - Title-page from the second edition of Thruston's The Antiquities of Tennessee. From the **author's collection.**

October 20, 1865 - The state prison on Church Street, where Champ Ferguson was hanged. Photo from **Art Work of Nashville.**

October 22, 1907 - President Theodore Roosevelt at the Hermitage. Photo courtesy of **Carl Zibart.**

October 28, 1843 - Title-page to Dr. John Sappington's book. Sappington was assisted in his efforts by Dr. Ferdinando Stith of Franklin. From the **author's collection.**

October 31, 1847 - A William Strickland masterpiece, St. Mary's Cathedral. Photo from **Art Work of Nashville.**

November 1, 1880 - Internationally known sportswriter, Grantland Rice (second from left), and Vanderbilt's Dan McGugin (right). Photo courtesy of **Carl Zibart.**

November 2, 1907 - Young man dressed to play football at the turn of the century. Photo courtesy of **Carl Zibart.**

November 5, 1912 - The Nashville Resorvoir on Eighth Avenue, South, at the turn of the century. Photo from **Art Work of Nashville.**

November 6, 1860 - Presidential candidate John Bell of Nashville. Drawing from **Harper's Pictorial History of the Civil War.**

November 20, 1863 - Sam Davis, boy hero.
*Drawing by **Jim Farrell**.*

November 27, 1890 - Sulphur Dell Baseball Park, located just north of the State
Capitol. *Photo courtesy of the **Tennessee State Library and Archives**.*

November 30, 1864 - The Carter gin house, scene of some of the bloodiest fighting
at Franklin. *Drawing from **Century Magazine**.*

December 1, 1890 - The Vine Street Christian Church.
*Photo from **Nashville, Tenn**. in **Photo-Gravure from Recent Negatives**.*

December 9, 1897 - John Berrien Lindsley.
*Portrait by **Cornelius Hankins, from John Berrien Lindsley**.*

December 13, 1919 - One of Gilbert Gaul's most popular works, Leaving Home.
*From the **author's collection**.*

December 15, 1864 - Plan of the Battle of Nashville.
*Map by **Dan Pomeroy**, from **Tennesseans at War**.*

December 19, 1840 - Felix Grundy, who, in his time, was one of the most influential
men in the United States. *Portrait from **The Pageant of America**.*

December 22, 1828 - Rachel Donelson Jackson. *Drawing by **Jim Farrell**.*

December 24, 1824 - One of the buildings comprising the University of Nashville
on present-day Second Avenue, South. *Photo from **Art Work of Nashville**.*

December 25, 1779 - The James Robertson party arriving at the site of Nashville.
*Painting by **Sandor Bodo**, courtesy of **First Tennessee Bank**.*

December 26, 1904 - The Ryman Auditorium shortly after it was renamed.
*Photo from **Nashville, the Gateway of the South**.*

December 30, 1926 - First Avenue, South and Broad Street during the 1926-1927
floods. *Photo courtesy of the **Nashville Public Library**.*